VINTAGE
FASHION
SOURCEBOOK

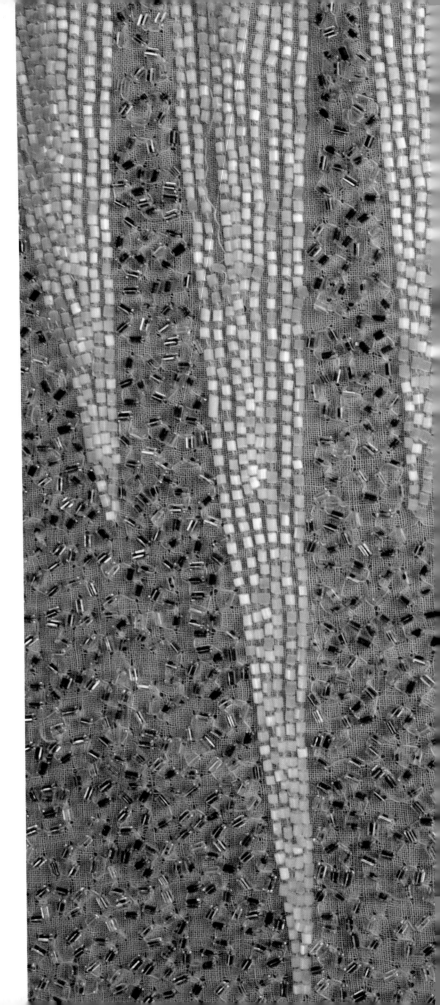

THIS IS A CARLTON BOOK

First published in 2006 by Carlton Books Limited,
20 Mortimer Street, London W1T 3JW

This abridged edition published in 2011.

10 9 8 7 6 5 4 3 2 1

A CIP catalogue record for this book
is available from the British Library

ISBN 978 1 84732 792 5

Printed and bound in China

Senior Executive Editor: Lisa Dyer
Senior Art Editor: Emma Wicks
Designer: Adam Wright
Copy Editors: Nicky Gyopari, Diana Craig and Libby Willis
Picture Researchers: Paul Langan and Jenny Meredith
Production: Caroline Alberti
Special Photography: Emma Wicks

Contents

introduction   4

1900-1929   6

1930s   14

1940s   20

1950s   26

1960s   32

1970s   38

1980s   46

shopping guide   52

collections & stores   56

glossary of designers   58

glossary of fashion terms   61

acknowledgements   64

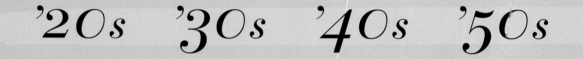

'20s '30s '40s '50s

Introduction

A historical record, a cherished possession, a personal belonging that may be described as a 'second skin': favourite items of clothing have the power to transform the body and spirit of women the world over and always have. The interest in vintage clothing ties deeply into this almost physical response to fashion. Vintage pieces capture not only a historical moment in time, but in themselves can be works of absolute and unique beauty. The techniques and handworking of previous decades, before mass production, can be seen on early pieces up until the end of the Second World War in 1945. After this, factories had learned to mass-produce clothes and a vast number of off-the-rack styles became available to the public. Gone were the days when a handful of couturiers set the pace for style and local seamstresses copied patterns from Paris or fashion magazines. In becoming reliant upon the manufacturers that produced the clothes, individuality was lost to some extent. However vintage pieces reclaim this by transcending the limitations of what's stylish or available today – a 1930s bias-cut Vionnet gown or a 1950s Christian Dior dress can be stand-out stunning any time. Why choose from the ready-to-wear options produced for you, when the whole history of fashion is available?

Several trends set in earlier decades have developed into classics: the shift dress, the twin set, the tailored suit, the bias-cut gown, the little black dress and many more have not drastically changed since their inception. Even today couture designers plunder the back catalogues in order to study, copy and learn from the masters of years before, often mimicking details, such as pin tucks or seam-finishing,

'60s '70s '80s

as well as prints, pattern-cuts or surface decoration, such as beading, lacework or ribbonwork, in their own designs.

In this book vintage pieces are charted through a framework of fashion history over ninety years of the last century, celebrating the most significant designers, developments and movements of each decade, which have contributed to fashion as we know it. Starting from the time when Parisian haute couture houses led the way at the onset of the twentieth century, four writers chronicle the arrival of the flapper, the 'make do and mend' fashions of the war years, Christian Dior's New Look, the 'Swinging '60s', punk and antifashion movements, new romanticism and the power-suited 1980s – all in examples of collectible vintage samples from the time. Giving an overview of changing trends, the book invests the reader with the knowledge necessary to identify pieces as belonging to specific time periods, to distinguish between various fashion movements, and to understand how and why certain fashions were worn at the time.

In many ways today's fashions evolve from the needs and desires of women rather than the social diktats, conventions and mores that once set the tone of the day. Although fashion has been liberated from the constraints of society and tradition, at this particular vantage point in the twenty-first century we can look back, learn and reinvent, taking what we like from fashions that have gone before, wearing clothing in different ways than originally intended, or simply collecting favourite pieces for the sheer unadulterated pleasure of owning something incomparably beautiful, rare and elusive.

1900-29

At the turn of the century, the Edwardian sun shone for a privileged few. Fashion was dictated from the top and the decorative female in her frills and flounces seemed to waft through society while caged in an ironclad corset. As modernism gathered pace, both the corset and the suffocating Victorian values of the time were torn apart, and in 1909 a new linear silhouette came into fashion. Societal norms were challenged, and an explosion of originality and progressive ideas in art, film, psychology and the role of women were established.

Ethnic elements – oriental themes, ancient Greece and Japanese prints – all influenced fashion, shown in exotic-styled motifs, the natural form and the curvilinear designs of the avant-garde. Added to this, following the tragedy of the First World War and post-1918 fashion, women went wild. Hemlines went up, waistlines went down and flappers boogied to the Charleston, the Bunny Hop and the new hot sound of jazz. Fringes, beads and tassels ornamented short dresses worn above the knee and the accent was on youth and 'misbehaving'.

By the 1920s the media age was beginning. People acquired their sartorial ideas not from their 'betters' but from listening to the radio, copying stars in the cinema and reading about the fashions in *Vogue* and *Vanity Fair*. The growing popularity of sports such as tennis and cycling prompted a new and simpler look. Jean Patou, Madeleine Vionnet and Coco Chanel were among the designers who created the first modern style for women still seen today.

◀Beading and fringing

Evening dresses with sequins, feathers and other ornate surface decorations were characteristic of the period, as in this fringed flapper dress seen here modelled by Joan Crawford in the 1920s.

The sheath dress

The slinky sheath was made of chiffon, silk or crepe de chine, and clung to the female form from shoestring shoulder straps.

▼Geometrics

Sweeping bold curved patterns in deep colours that included dramatic red, black and blue appeared from 1910, along with other geometric patterns and Cubist motifs.

Key looks of the era
1900-1929

Edwardian blouses

The Edwardian blouse, made of lace with ruffles, or striped and purposeful, epitomized the dual femininity – both demure and assertive – of the times.

S-shaped corsets

The early-century corset created the idealized female form with a tiny waist – achieved through artificial distortion of the body.

Style Russe

Chanel's early 1920s Russian style, attributed to her liaison with Russian Grand Duke Dmitri, consisted of tunic shapes, fur trimmings and embroideries. This look reflected the influx of Russians to Paris after the Revolution. 'Style Russe' would be revisited by many designers, as in Saint Laurent's 'Russian Revolution' in the mid-1970s.

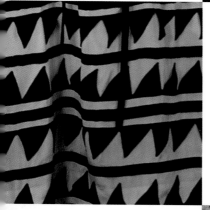

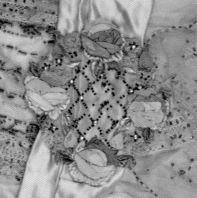

▲Hobble and kite dresses

After the emancipation from the strict *belle époque* silhouette, dresses became looser while the 'hobble', as created by Paul Poiret, was groundbreaking in developing the narrow, shorter hemline – an influence that can be seen in these kite dresses from 1918. Lace-up boots also came back into fashion during the years of the First World War.

Dropped waist

...rves and the hourglass figure ...re out, and belts, sashes or ...s were worn around the hips. ...e waist disappeared to create ...e fashionable beanpole look ...oved in the '20s, as typified ...the illustration from Mab ...tterns, April 1925, below.

Le Garçonne look

A new androgyny accompanied the flapper era, and women wore short hair and dresses that were straight, loose and revealed bare arms. The lithe, athletic, modern form was the new sexy look.

Velvets and furs

Fur coats, or coats trimmed in fur, were popular. Many had a single large button, or wrapped over, a shawl collar, wide cuffs and fell to the knees. Velvet was also used in jackets, wraps and dresses; the sumptuous material was part of the style of opulence and the luxury of Art Deco fashion.

▲Kimono style

Japanese-style dresses were seen as very exotic and heralded a new form of beauty based on simplicity and oriental design. Many teagowns, like the 1925 dress above, had the square-cut sleeves and shape of the kimono.

▲Bare backs and bias cuts

Cut on the bias, the new body-hugging dresses seemed to spiral round the body and moved with the wearer. Backless dresses, like the 1929 version above, with or without trains, began to make an appearance later in the 1920s.

Sweaters

Silk or wool, and striped, plain or with *trompe l'oeil* motifs, the jumper was a key element in flapper style of the 1920s.

Trousers

Bright young things in the 1920s would wear silken pyjamas and sailor pants for early evening or as fashionable resort wear.

ABOVE LEFT AND RIGHT
Beaded gold and cream
straight-line 1926 flapper
dress, without and with the
cardigan. The geometric
diamond design is classic
Art Deco. The neckline is a
V-neck with fill-in and the
irregular hem falls to the
knees, typical of the period.

The Age of the Flapper

By 1924 the wise-cracking flappers were as much known for their reckless behaviour as for their style. Smoking and putting their make-up on in public, the bright young things drank and danced the Shimmy and the Bunny Hop in a frenzy of excitement. Taping up their breasts to get rid of unwanted curves, they looked youthful and boyish, and the new silhouette was slender, straight up and down like a board, and in fact became known as 'le garçonne'.

As if to herald the new mood, the waistline dropped dramatically in 1925 to below the hip, and by 1927 it had disappeared altogether and the hemline risen a scandalous 38 cm (15 in) to just below the knee. The flapper look was at its apogee and extremely short skirts were worn day and night. But hemlines crashed down along with Wall Street in 1929, just as waistlines and busts edged their way into fashion consciousness.

Flapper dresses were straight, loose and sleeveless, revealing a new body awareness. Arms were bare, and legs and backs were exposed for the first time, becoming new erogenous zones. The illusion of nudity was heightened by the use of diaphanous fabrics and little adornment. Beading was used to emphasize the see-through materials and catch the light, yet also highlighted the risqué nature of the outfits.

The short shift dress, which fell straight down from the shoulders and stopped above the knees, dominated the mid- to late 1920s. Ornamented with geometric and abstract designs, the chemise was often beaded with bands of glittering sequins.

For daywear the three-piece jersey suit was the cornerstone of female fashion: a blouse worn with a patterned or plain knitted sweater or a Chanel-style cardigan jacket with pockets was teamed with a narrow, short, pleated skirt. Day dresses were simple or decorated with details such as horizontal tucks, seaming or bias-cut panels and square boatnecks. Combinations of fabrics were used and two-tones,

LEFT AND BELOW RIGHT
Molyneux orange silk 1925 dress with silver and gold embroidery. Even on flapper dresses Molyneux's designs were more minimalist than those of his contemporaries – robust fabrics, strong modernist motifs and a perfect cut made them demanding though utterly elegant pieces.

SIGNATURE FLAPPER ELEMENTS:

- Uneven split hems and handkerchief points that are longer at the back
- Egyptian- and Art-Deco-inspired motifs
- Visible seam decoration and double seams
- Diagonal lines and asymmetric trimmed necklines
- Pockets, buttons and belts
- Pleated panels on skirts and knife pleats
- Day dresses belted around the hips
- Low-cut necks and backs, with thin straps
- Narrow trailing scarves, sometimes attached to dresses

graded shades were popular, as were mannish suits, ties and small geometric prints.

A pioneer with Coco Chanel of the 'garçonne' look, Jean Patou designed sports ensembles with gradating stripes that could be worn with his geometric jumpers and cardigans on the Riviera. He designed beige three-piece jersey suits, dresses and wraps. His afternoon flapper-style crepe dresses had self-tied shoulder bows or decorative seams worked in zig-zags.

The bright young things wore trousers at home in the early evenings or at the beach. Loosely cut with drawstring or elasticated waists, they were sometimes called Oxford Bags and fastened at the side for modesty. Paquin's Chinese-printed satin pyjamas with embroidered satin jacket were all the rage.

The perfectly straight-line collarless coat that buttoned at the waist like a cardigan jacket and a high-collar coat with a sash at the waist maintained their popularity, as did the slightly circular coat with fur collar that wrapped over on the diagonal, fastening with a single loop and button at hip level.

Eveningwear

The modern social whirl of cabarets, fancy dress parties and dancing gave rise to more extravagant evening wear. And by 1928 Paris was determined to abandon the tubular dresses, and floating panels and Vionnet's bias-cut dresses, which followed the contours of the body, became popular. Draperies from the hips gave the illusion of length and fullness, and movement was added with attached panels or uneven hemlines. Chanel's black evening dresses with huge transparent draperies, Paquin's acid-green moiré dresses with a V-neck and bulk at the hip, and Molyneux's transparent printed dresses with full, scalloped skirts and arm draperies are all significant flapper styles.

Crystal-beaded waves with coral fish and lilac flamingos in lotus ponds were some of Molyneux's unconventional surface decoration on flapper dresses. He experimented with ostrich feathers and buttons resembling cigarette butts or lipsticks, and his beaded chemises are some of the most exquisite.

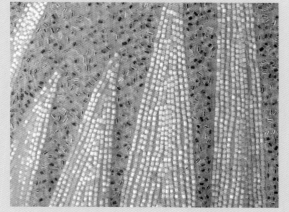

ABOVE Silver lamé flower-patterned Erté-style dress with a flower corsage at the waist, early 1920s.

LEFT AND ABOVE RIGHT Cream and white 1925 beaded flapper dress in starburst Art Deco design.

1930s

Epitomized by the elongated draped gowns worn by movie stars, the 1930s will for ever be remembered as the era of Hollywood glamour. Liberated from the corsets and cumbersome designs of previous years, women were now able to dress in a way that was both stylish and practical, while new fabrics encouraged designers to experiment with original looks.

Form was more important than detail and embellishment as designers focused on the silhouette. Unlike the boyish 1920s when breasts were strapped down and dresses were loose and boxy, clothes were cut to follow the lines of the body, showing off the female figure in a more provocative manner than ever before. Shoulders were bared in the first halterneck and backless gowns, and the bias-cut dress – pioneered by Parisian couturier Madeleine Vionnet – clung to every curve. Suits consisted of neat-fitting, waist-length jackets with skirts to mid-calf. Coco Chanel designed two-piece suits in wool jersey fabrics, which heralded a sportier look that became a surprise daywear hit.

However, many of these new trends were born of necessity. Coming between the two world wars and directly after the stock market crash of 1929, times were hard. The Great Depression meant that designers had to work with cheaper materials and ordinary women could no longer afford the sartorial excesses of previous decades. Even the wealthiest showed restraint in what they wore, while screen idols such as Katharine Hepburn and Bette Davis represented a glamour that most could only dream of.

▼ Bias-cut gowns
Fabric was cut on the diagonal, allowing dresses to cling naturally to the body. Introduced by Madeleine Vionnet, this was one of the most significant elements of 1930s fashion. Below a black velvet dress trimmed in ermine and a white crepe and panne velvet dress, both by Vionnet, circa 1930.

▶ Skirts with wedge-cut pleats
Fitted at the hip with yokes, skirts often featured wedge-cut pleats giving a fullness to the hemline, which ended at mid-calf. The fashion pictured here also exhibits other classic 1930s styles: hat and gloves, neckline bow and fur stole.

Rayon
The first commercially used man-made fabric was available in several different finishes and was quickly exploited by designers keen to experiment with new textiles.

Key looks of the decade

1930s

Jabot blouse
Decorative frills cascaded from the collar down the front of the blouse or dress, becoming a popular style, particularly for daywear.

▶ Sportswear influences
Tailoring took on a sportier feel Coco Chanel pioneered the use of soft wool jersey fabrics for women's suiting. More women engaged in outdoor activities and such athletics as golfing. Here four women play golf wearing beach pyjamas in 1935.

◀ Flared sleeves
Narrow-fitting at the shoulder, blouses featured sleeves which widened towards the wrist. These were often exaggerated and elongated on evening gowns.

Costume jewellery

Often made in enamel and glass, costume jewellery such as brooches, bracelets and beaded necklaces were a fashionable and affordable new look.

Narrow suits worn with a hat and gloves

Slim-fitting tailored suits were a practical look for daywear and were teamed with gloves and hats of various styles.

Zips

Slide fasteners were a welcomed new invention, which quickly replaced buttons in many areas of fashion. Some designers, such as Schiaparelli, even made features of this metal fastening.

◄ Halterneck backless evening gowns

Backs became the new erogenous zone as designers draped fabric around the neck, leaving shoulders and backs on show, as seen here in a 1935 satin version.

▲ Art Deco patterns

Characterized by symmetrical geometric patterns, Art Deco prints were a left-over trend from the 1920s and were regularly seen on dresses, blouses and scarves.

◄ Fur

Worn day and night, fur creations of all types were popular luxury items. Capes, coats, stoles and wraps were made using pelts of ermine, fox, mink and chinchilla. This ermine version from 1935 has a draped collar.

Daywear Fashions

Until the 1930s daywear had often been more decorative than practical. But now, for the first time, women of all social backgrounds were beginning to lead busier and more productive lives and so clothes became easy to wear and unrestrictive. Although eveningwear had a strong element of escapist glamour, by day elegant and tidy clothes were key.

Money was tight, so women were no longer at liberty to indulge their every fashion fancy and had to find other ways to look smart. Clothes were mended instead of replaced and accessories played an important part. Costume jewellery, especially brooches, earrings and rings, was favoured as a cheaper alternative to the priceless gems that had previously been the required jewellery among the fashionable classes. Fine leather gloves in nubuck or lambskin also added an essential touch to daywear. Hats were worn at a fashionable tilt, and while the beret replaced the cloche hat, pillboxes also became popular and the turban emerged as one of the most glamorous accessories of the time.

As the decade progressed, function became more and more important, and by the time the Second World War had begun in 1939, simple clothes such as trousers, sweaters, classic shirtwaisters and low-heeled shoes were the staple of most women's wardrobes. Designers began to adapt the mood of their collections to more military-inspired, square-shouldered clothing, with skirts that hung just below the knee and often slightly longer at the back.

But this new liking for practical day clothes did not mean that fashion had lost its femininity – on the contrary, designers compensated by creating a more hourglass silhouette. Instead of sitting low on the hips as they had in the 1920s, waistlines returned to the natural waist, if not slightly higher, and were often cinched-in to create a more curvaceous figure. Necklines were lowered and

frequently had wide scalloped edges and ruffled collars, while the jabot blouse – with its ornamental cascade of frills down the front – became hugely fashionable, as did the pussy-bow neckline.

Flamboyant floral and geometric prints were favourites for blouses and day dresses, while the most fashionable colours of the time were powder blue, maize, grey, navy, green, brown and red. Rose was popular among teenage girls, while black was generally reserved for eveningwear.

Accents were important, too: belts and sashes were wide, buttons were bold and silk flowers were substantial, yet always in proportion to the jacket or dress they were adorning.

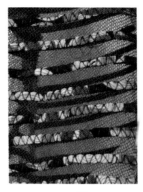

ABOVE AND LEFT Blouse with jabot collar and trumpet sleeves by Edward Molyneux, mid-1930s. The sleeves are worked with a rouleau detail of fabric, in which the material is robed and applied to net, a typical 1930s techique.

PAGE 14 White organza 1938 bridesmaid's dress sprinkled with flowers by Jeanne Lanvin, worn with a wide-brimmed organza hat with streamers, in front of a backdrop of line drawings of moths.

OPPOSITE A 1932 illustration depicting 1930s day dresses by, from left to right, Goupy, Worth, Augustabernard and Schiaparelli.

1940s

Social trends dictate fashion. Nowhere is this more evident than in the 1940s. With the outbreak of war, things changed very quickly. There were shortages of everything and civilian life was taken over and transformed. The conscription of women in Europe and America changed the female role and brought the woman out of the home to be directed in war work. Materials like silk and wool were needed for the war effort, factories were used for parachutes and other war supplies, so many of the 1940s vintage clothes are made out of rayon, synthetic jersey and other manmade fabrics. In 1941 clothing rationing came in and the government Utility scheme forbade the use of trimmings and certain materials as fashion was subject to government decree. The nonfashion fashion of the war years resulted in a conservative and military style, yet the tailoring was magnificent – outfits had to last several seasons. British couture was still being made, but only for export to procure much-needed dollars for armaments. France lost its position at the apex of fashion in 1940 under German occupation and did not regain its undisputed leadership until the liberation in 1944 when its couture collection was splendid. Meanwhile, America looked to its own designers to create fashions; the functional and easy American ready-to-wear was born with brightly coloured playsuits in materials like gingham, cotton and denim. After the war, the direction of fashion was slow to change, especially where rationing was still in place. The American softened silhouette presaged the dramatic New Look unveiled in 1947 by Christian Dior and the mood changed irrevocably.

▼ Slacks

All styles of slacks, especially pioneer pants, became popular as women got used to wearing trousers at work. Here actress Lilli Palmer is shown in 1946 wearing her man-tailored grey gabardine slacks, along with a beige suede jacket.

▶ Sequins and beads

Not rationed by the war, sequins were sewn on dresses, jackets and shawls to add sparkle to daywear and eveningwear. This 1945 white crepe gown, covered with bugle beads, and with dolman sleeves is by New York costume designer Kiviette.

Utility suit

Clothing by law. Designed along tailored lines in military-style boxy jacket and narrow, short skirt, they were most often made in blues, blacks and browns.

Key looks of the decade

1940s

▶ Trench coats

Military styling was evident in jackets and coats during the war years; here a red wool belted trench coat, lined in black rabbit, is by Traina-Norell, 1943. Bell-shaped coats with large collars were also popular.

▲ Gingham

America's favourite fabric. Shirtdresses and pinafores all had a fresh new look in gingham, which became popular during the war years. This 1947 blue gingham dress is worn with a red gingham scarf and red kid shoes.

ructured couture gowns in
in featured elaborate detailing
d were made in unforgiving
rics like velvet, and heavy
in and faille. Greek-inspired
eath dresses based on the toga
de use of pleated chiffon in
on crepe and greige.

nastic dress
osely fitted and shaped like a
uminous tent, the dress was
en a soft shape when belted.

Peasant dress
Exotic handwoven printed
skirts and off-the-shoulder
blouses with drawstring
necklines and puffed sleeves
were popularized, partly due
to the success of the Brazilian
bombshell, Carmen Miranda.

▶Bolero jacket
Short and emphasizing the
waist, with padded shoulders and
shirring, the bolero was often worn
over strapless evening dresses.
Here a navy bolero is worn with a
white blouse and red skirt – classic
patriotic colours – in 1942.

rsey shift dress
mple and elegant, the shift was
hortish unstructured design in
thetic jersey, which was made
ular by New York designers,
h as Norman Norell.

Rayon print dress
Pretty for daytime wear in the
new noncrease rayon fabric,
dresses exhibited colourful prints,
often with shirring and draping
on the bodice or waist.

▲Sportswear and beach
Summer dresses and midriff-
baring tops with matching shorts
were influenced by outdoor
athletics, as in this 1946 day
dress by Claire McCardell.

The Wartime Silhouette

Il faut 'skimp' pour etre chic', – you must skimp to be chic – declared *Vogue* in October 1941, referring to the tight, short-skirted silhouette that was ushered in that year and welcomed with horror by the public. Suddenly the flirty fullness of the 1930s curvy female gave way to an angular, hard silhouette that, as *Vogue* declared in the same year, 'would be brutally unbecoming unless women kept their figures'. Driven by the wartime economy, the sculptural silhouette was the result of government rationing. The stiff tailoring, economy of cut, nipped-in waist and narrow skirts produced a slim shape that de-emphasized the female curves and made the form appear slender yet mannish. Elaboration was out and pared-down elegance was the order of the day. The silhouette therefore, inadvertently gave the illusion of brisk competence. And with its 'sensible' image, 'beauty' was not part of the wartime aesthetic. *Vogue* said in 1942 that it looked, 'Sharp, cold and even bold'.

The ladies' suit

The drab uniformity of the war years was mirrored in the severe military-cut suit, which formed the bedrock of wartime fashion. Women wore clothes that were cut along the lines of the uniforms worn by men. Monochrome colours such as air-force blue and flag red were used, as these reduced wastage. Military influences were everywhere, from half-belts like those on uniform great coats to the padded-shoulder severity of wartime jackets. *Vogue* called it 'couture austerity'. Driven by necessity rather than by desire, restrictions on materials resulted in a silhouette that became refined and unadorned. Indeed, it was unpatriotic to be concerned with flounces and fripperies.

The suit was cut in a straight mannish style – often refashioned from the existing male suit – with sharp-edged shoulder pads to give women a brisk no-nonsense air, in keeping with their role as key wartime workers. Boxy, with wide shoulders and barely nipped in waists, the jackets were short, at 63.5 cm (25 in) or less in length. Single-breasted and often unlined in order to comply with fabric restrictions, they were, however, tailored and well made as they had to last several seasons. If they were lined, it was often with rayon. To save material, cuffs and patch pockets were banned in America as part of a 'no fabric on fabric' rule. Sometimes jacket sleeves were cropped short to reveal the blouse underneath and belts buckled at the back to leave the front smooth. The buttons, restricted to three or less, were often covered in the corresponding suit material.

As wool was impossible to come by, new materials like jersey wool, thick heavy rayon and crepe took their place. Despite what seems like an era of drab uniformity, a lot of the 1940s non-Utility suits have clever detailing. Clever panelling, set in different ways, in corded material for example, and crenellated yokes, added a dash of variety to the standard fare. Soft velveteen suits were fashionable and had gored skirts, accompanied by an unlined cardigan or jacket with a blouse feel. The outfit was completed with platform heels, often in cork or wood.

After the war, the female silhouette, while remaining slim, started to show changes. A softer line was creeping in with jackets losing the military cut. Gathered and curved-in waistlines, scalloped shoulders and gathered sleeves were seen in the Sears catalogue in 1946 and *Vogue* featured Parisian suits with hip-draped skirts and coat frocks with stand-up collars.

PAGE 20 Red checked dress in spun rayon, 1943. Two staples of the time, rayon and gingham, are used in this 1940s dress with three-quarter-length sleeves, necktie bow and hip pockets. The model stands in front of an Uncle Sam recruitment poster for the US armed forces.

LEFT Grey wool suit with red trim by American label Foxbrownie, 1944. Foxbrownie (or Fox-Brownie, as it is sometimes seen) was formed in 1937 by designer Stella Brownie and partner William Fox.

RIGHT Model wearing a Vogue pattern by Pierre Balmain, 1949. By this point in the decade, a more nipped-in hourglass shape was emerging. Balmain set up on his own in 1945, and designed elegant, feminine daywear, reaching his zenith with luxurious gowns and costumes for Hollywood starlets.

1950s

The 1950s kicked off with a feeling of hope and euphoria following the conclusion of the Second World War, and the generally rapturous applause that had greeted Dior's New Look in 1947. In Great Britain the government promised to 'Make Britain Great Again', and immediately set to work on the Festival of Britain exhibition that took place on the South Bank of the Thames in 1951. There was a significantly optimistic outlook for the world in general, and that included the fashion industry. After years of hardship and drudgery, when women had worn sexless, utilitarian work garments (and when there were fewer men around to impress), there was an understandable desire to dress up in luxurious feminine clothes. While Britain itself was almost bankrupt and rationing dragged on until 1954, the sheer extravagance of Dior's New Look seemed to point to a future of confidence and prosperity, something that everyone aspired to. Dior's designs were to dominate, but not everyone was thrilled; for some Dior seemed out of tune with postwar Europe and a symbol of luxury, extravagance – some of his skirts required 18 m (20 yards) of material – and privilege that many hoped the war had destroyed. Times had definitely changed. For all the hardships and tragedies that women had dealt with during the war, it had in fact been a time of liberation and equality. Hundreds of young women had been freed from the domesticity of housework and sent out to work as land girls, driving ambulances or in munitions factories. The idea that fashion now intended them to revert to a romantic notion of femininity with a padded bosom and nipped-in waist, was something many were not prepared for.

▼Gloves

Women wore short kid leather gloves for formal daywear, and in the evening long satin gloves were worn to complement their strapless cocktail dresses and evening gowns. The fashionable look was to wear them pushed down with big glitzy bracelets over the top.

Slacks

Old-fashioned, ski-pant-style trousers were made from synthetic stretch fabric in plain fabrics or multicoloured plaid. Tailored to fit the body, they had a flat front waistband and side zip opening; they epitomized the casual look in America's growing leisurewear market.

▶Ballet shoes

Simple flat black pumps based on a classic ballet shoe became popular in 1950s America and Europe. They were mass produced and worn with ankle socks and full skirts, or with bare feet and cut-off capri pants.

▼Net petticoats

Layers of petticoats were worn under full skirts to give lift and movement; they were stiffened with starch or a sugar solution to keep their form. Tiered petticoats made from nylon tulle gave a softer look that was less ballroom-dancing in style. They gave form and volume to many styles of 1950s ballgowns.

Key looks of the decade

1950s

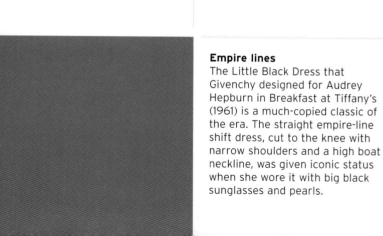

Hats

Pull-down bucket hats, small lampshade-style hats, coolie hats and wide-brimmed flat picture hats made from coloured straw were all popular shapes. Black and white were used to graphic effect and for grand occasions, and women often wore a formal black net veil.

Pencil skirts

A narrow, slim straight skirt called the 'hobble', and first pioneered by Poiret, restricted women's walking. It fell from a narrow waistband with little excess fabric, no gathers or pleats and usually a small back split that allowed for movement.

Empire lines

The Little Black Dress that Givenchy designed for Audrey Hepburn in Breakfast at Tiffany's (1961) is a much-copied classic of the era. The straight empire-line shift dress, cut to the knee with narrow shoulders and a high boat neckline, was given iconic status when she wore it with big black sunglasses and pearls.

Fur stoles

The most popular style of eveningwear was strapless, and the addition of a large fur stole wrapped around bare shoulders, sometimes fastened with a large brooch, became the most fashionable way to keep covered in the evening.

rsized detailing

decade's tailoring embraced
rsized details in the form of
e shawl collars, giant buttons
big turn-back cuffs on wide
are-cut sleeves with very
p armholes, known as
nan sleeves.

Trapeze coats

The loose swing coat, that was
sometimes called a 'tent' and
resembled a triangle in shape,
was made to accommodate the
wide skirts of the time, and the
post-war pregnancy boom. Many
were given a diverging set of
buttons designed to emphasize
the triangle shape of the cut.

◀Sack dress

The waistless Givenchy Sack
dress, as modelled here by
Audrey Hepburn in 1958, finally
freed the figure from the
restrictive hourglass.

Sheath dress

The fitted sheath clung to a
woman's body shape. In satin or
silk, it was usually strapless and
required considerable corseting.

Wide belts

A small waist was emphasized
for almost every fashionable look
throughout the decade. Either
with a full dirndl skirt or a straight
pencil skirt, or with sporty slacks
or capri pants, a big wide belt was
a must-have fashion accessory.

dal pushers and capris

-length trousers, either
ed or flounced at the hem
ut narrow, were prominant
high street to high fashion.
ris were slimline pant and
t had a small V at the hem
hable greater mobility.
e Natalie Wood models
apless top and pedal
ers in the 1950s.

▲Full skirts

Wide circular skirts were worn
for daywear in simple fabrics like
gingham and printed cottons.
They sometimes had a big
bold design, like a poodle or
American cowboy motifs, printed
on them. For eveningwear full
skirts were made from layers
of frothy chiffon or rayon in the
most vibrant of colours – canary
yellow, baby blue and lime green.

Sweater dressing

The short-sleeved turtleneck
worn tight and fitted, and the big
bulky pastel-coloured sweater
were favourites for teenagers
and movie stars alike. The
invention of the twinset, with
its sleeveless crew-necked vest
and matching cardigan with neat
pearl buttons and decorative
beading, became a 1950s staple,

Fit or Flounce Silhouettes

PAGE 26 Model wearing a Balenciaga evening dress and wrap with a black hat, and diamonds by Van Cleef & Arpels, 1952. Balenciaga was noted for his refined elegance; his gigantic flounces and sculptural cutting created a frame for the body.

BELOW Taffeta shantung dresses in the New Look shape, 1951. Coordinating hats and gloves were very much part of the polished look of the period.

The 1950s was the last decade when Paris still dominated worldwide fashion. Dior was unstoppable, and he remained influential until his death in 1957; alongside him were other great designers determined to succeed. Cristobal Balenciaga, Jacques Fath and Hubert de Givenchy were all leading names of the era, but the clock was ticking and as the decade unfolded there were signs that the elitism of haute couture was starting to lose its dominance. The decade was a transitional one that moved from the austerity of the 1940s to the prosperity of the 1960s; in fact, the dividing line was becoming clearer by 1956 with the increasing influence of the teenager youth culture in America, and the identification of the young as a separate consumer group.

The decade will be remembered mainly for two contrasting silhouettes, although there were myriad alternative shapes (not all of which were hugely successful) that flourished briefly and then disappeared. The great full skirt that swirled and sashayed and the slim pencil tubular skirt that fell to the knee were quintessential silhouettes, and both placed great emphasis on the narrowness of the waist. After the miserable war years, women were eager to embrace the femininity. Strategic padding and structured underwear did much to improve a less-than-perfect body, so that Dior's extreme silhouette of

1951/52 – Ligne Longue

1952 – Ligne Sinueuse

1952/53 – L

Tulipe

1953/54 – Ligne Vivante

1954 – Ligne Muguet

1954/55 – Ligne H

1955 – Ligne A

1955/56 – Ligne Y

1956 – Ligne Flèche

nipped-in waist and swirling mid-calf skirt could look fabulous on everyone. The nylon all-in-one corselet gave a waspish waist, pulled in the hips and shunted the breasts upwards and outwards to give a perfect hourglass figure, as seen in Anita Ekberg in Fellini's *La Dolce Vita*. Fashion was still dictating rigid and uncomfortable dress codes, and women continued to fall into line as they wanted to appear alluring and sophisticated.

Women everywhere fell in love with the glamorous clothes of the time, chronicled as the 'fashion-conscious '50s'. An elegant appearance required the correct accessories, and smart women were still expected to wear hats, gloves and matching shoes and handbag to be considered well dressed. Although functionality and simplicity were increasingly prevalent in daywear (easy separates and sporty slacks reflected an increased interest in athletics), eveningwear was dramatically show-stopping, with long gloves, high heels and drop earrings essential to complete the look. Hair was worn high on the head, in variations of a Dusty Springfield beehive, or cut short to the face in a gamine Jean Seberg crop.

Dior's hourglass figure was not the only silhouette of the decade though, and he himself experimented with many other shapes; almost every Dior collection saw the introduction of a new silhouette – the Princess line, the A-line, the H-line and the S-line all followed each other in quick succession. Dior's invention of the A-line was quite simply a dress that fell from fitted shoulders outwards towards the hem and used stiffened fabric to create the shape. The A-line and the H-line were offering women even more choice and another set of vastly contrasting shapes were hailed as the latest look.

The waistline started to fluctuate, changes in length and line came in quick succession, and women were expected to keep up with many innovative directions. Skirts ranged from voluminous fullness through neat tailored pleats to snug slimline pencils. The Sack, Princess, Tulip and Trapeze lines were all to come and go before the end of the decade, as designers seemed to waver between very structured clothes that could almost support themselves and clothes that were much more fluid and relied on the female body to provide form and shape.

ABOVE Almost every Christian Dior collection of the decade featured a new silhouette, though all kept a narrow waist and a below-knee hemline.

1960s

The Swinging '60s, as they became known, heralded an extraordinary decade of change after the austerity and reconstruction of the 1950s. The fashion zeitgeist was changing direction and whereas in previous generations it was always Paris that had led the way, now the whole world looked to London. When in 1960 a 24-year-old Yves Saint Laurent showed what was to be his final collection for Christian Dior, and sent out a cool Beat collection of black leather suits and knitted caps to an astonished and slightly bewildered audience, he effectively sounded the death knell of French haute couture. With the rumblings of a revolution well under way in a party atmosphere in London, this was a defining moment when fashion turned a corner. Labels such as 'formal' and 'casual' dressing, which existed in the previous decade, ceased to have any meaning at all. As new styles arrived in small London boutiques on a weekly basis, the savvy shopper quickly learnt that fresh stock was delivered in the evenings and they hung around to make sure they were first to grab the latest looks. It was in the 1960s that fashion became absolutely central to a young person's identity. For the first time ever there was a generation of young people with money to spend, looking for ways to express their newfound sense of freedom through fashion, music and lifestyle. The generational power balance had shifted: young people were making things happen for themselves and taking great pleasure in doing so, while simultaneously thumbing their noses at the old-guard Establishment.

▶Space Age looks

With the moon landing came an avalanche of Space Age clothes, best exemplified by Courrèges with his all-white 'moon girl' collection in 1964. Space-inspired helmets in felted wool or white leather completed the look, as modelled here by Audrey Hepburn, 1965, in Courrèges.

Miniskirts

André Courrèges in Paris and Mary Quant in London can both lay claim to the invention of the mini skirt. Hemlines started creeping higher at the start of the decade, but by 1965 they had risen to mid-thigh and were to become even shorter. Often worn with a big belt hung loosely over the hips, they were adopted by women across the world, not just the young and leggy.

Hosiery

Innovations in the textile industry saw the invention of all-in-one nylon tights, which gave women much more freedom than stockings and suspenders. With the emphasis firmly directed on to the leg, tights quickly became an integral part of the look and were made in strong colours with thick stripes, printed patterns, diamonds and plaid for winter, while white lacy versions were worn under summer dresses.

Key looks of the decade

1960s

▼Graphic lines

Mini skirts, shift dresses and short A-line coats were all given the Op Art look as fashion reflected the optical illusions of Bridget Riley's paintings. Thick and thin stripes and geometric checks were used to create strong graphic impact in many of the pared-down simple shapes. Here Natalie Wood models Yves Saint Laurent's Mondrian dress.

▲Synthetics

Polyester, nylon and other manmade fabrics permitted the wearer movement even with slim-cut styles. This 1966 dress by New York designer Gayle Kirkpatrick, modelled by actress Pamela Tiffin, was made in a special stretch nylon developed by Stretchnit.

▲Boots

It was a decade of boots in various shapes and styles. Sh patent boots that came up to and over the knee in black, w and silver were the trendiest footwear to go with the mini. The other strong boot shape, which originated from Paris, a mid-calf white kidskin boot with a pointy toe and no heel sometimes with a flat ribbon bow around the top.

Chainmail

[P]o Rabanne's resolutely [mo]dern designs were made [i]n a variety of unconventional [mat]erials. Plastic chainmail and [alumi]nium appeared in silver, [blac]k or white. Difficult to work [wit]h, chainmail projected a [futu]ristic image that was very [mu]ch in tune with what women [wan]ted. The chainmail and mesh [cats]uit below twins chainmail [with] the trend for transparency.

Psychedelia

By the middle to late 1960s the emphasis had shifted from London to America, and more specifically to the flower children of San Francisco, with their anti-Vietnam chants, long hair and ragbag of utilitarian and ethnic garments. Brocade jeans, frilly shirts, flower-print tunics, Mao jackets and Indian scarves became a street style emulated by most European designers.

Sheer and transparent

Bodies became the centre of attention with transparent panels of clear plastic or mesh like netting, as in the chainmail catsuit below. Towards the end of the decade see-through clothes became more daring with Yves Saint Laurent's sheer black chiffon blouse and Ossie Clark's gossamer-fine chiffon dresses showing more barely covered flesh than ever before.

▶Plastics

Shiny PVC was used for every item of clothing from over-the-knee boots to mini macs, bags and pinafore dresses. It was easy to colour and to overprint with bold motifs. Connecting circles of hard plastic were popular for belts and earrings. Shown here, Paco Rabanne works vinyl, plastic and steel into a flowery 1967 dress.

Oversized sunglasses

Huge bug-eyed spectacles in shiny black or white plastic were one of the hottest accessories to match Op Art and Space Age styles. Perfectly round and goggle-like, they were worn more for photographic styling and celebrity 'disguise' than for everyday streetwear.

Maxi and midi lengths

Long coats, skirts and dresses were designed as the antidote to the mini. The maxi fell to the ankle, and the midi was cut to mid-calf. Women were given much more choice to decide what length they felt comfortable in, and they often chose to wear both at the same time: midi knit cardigans were worn over short skirts with boots to show a fleeting glimpse of leg.

[Cu]t-outs

[Sha]pes cut out of dresses [were] especially to reveal the [midri]ff section. Here a 1965 design [by J]ohn Bates teams a simple [shift] dress with cut-out stockings [deco]rated with roses and bows.

Shift dresses

The most popular shape was an A-line shift that fell in a clean triangular line from shoulder to mid-thigh. Big circular pockets, cutaway armholes and contrast edging around the neck, hem and armholes were defining features. Some were designed to wear over a skinny rib sweater and ribbed tights during the day, or to wear on their own with heels in the evening.

The British Explosion

Britain, and London in particular, was where everyone wanted to be, and the 'Youthquake' explosion that affected every area of popular culture gathered pace as the decade wore on. It was a time when young talented people, regardless of class or background, were determined to make revolutionary changes and demand recognition for what they did. Image was everything; fresh-faced photographers such as David Bailey, Terence Donovan and Brian Duffy changed the style of photography from formal studio-based portraiture to energetic street-style 'reality'. The models they worked with – Twiggy, Jean Shrimpton ('the Shrimp') and Verushka – became icons of their time for their playful poses and quirky looks.

The Beatles and the Rolling Stones changed the look and sound of music, and on the streets there were new and exciting boutiques springing up in Carnaby Street and the King's Road. Typically small, dark and deafeningly loud with the current pop music of the day, they flourished overnight and in many cases simply disappeared just as quickly. Owned and run by ambitious individuals, they were united by the weirdest of names: Granny Takes A Trip, Mr Freedom, Hung On You and I Was Lord Kitchener's Valet. Fashion was no longer dictated by middle-aged Parisian designers, and the demand by London's young 'dolly birds' to wear whatever they wanted, whenever and wherever they felt like it, was being met by a host of up-and-coming British design stars who were spilling out from art schools. The Royal College of Art Fashion Department was run by Professor Jayney Ironside, who became a legendary figure for her ability to spot and nurture a generation of young talents, many of whom went on to become internationally famous. Zandra Rhodes, Bill Gibb, Ossie Clark, Marion Foale and Sally Tuffin were all students under her tutorage. These and many others – including Gina Fratini, Anthony Price, Yuki and Thea Porter – were part of a mushrooming band of designers who were responsible for turning London into a leading fashion capital. Not all the bright young things who were helping to build Britain's fashionable reputation had a fashion degree; some had simply arrived at the same place by a different route.

Mary Quant, undoubtedly an early trailblazer of the Youthquake movement, had studied illustration at Goldsmiths, before setting up a tiny shop in 1955 with her then boyfriend and business partner Alexander Plunkett-Green. Barbara Hulanicki, the owner and designer behind the hugely influential Biba boutiques, started out as a fashion illustrator before deciding to try designing something she liked instead of illustrating other people's clothes. Jean Muir, who went on to become one of the leading British names for understated classics, started out as a sketcher for Jaeger.

PAGE 32 Model, muse and icon Twiggy in a gold-and-orange striped minidress in the 1960s.

OPPOSITE A 1960s advertisement for Mary Quant dresses in the new synthetic Courtelle. The classic minidress featured a zip down the front with a circular pull-ring.

RIGHT AND BELOW Mary Quant's Prince-of-Wales check dress for Ginger Group. This was made for her less expensive, mass-produced line of coordinates in 1963. Her miniskirt and 'Chelsea Look' became the most defining fashion features of the decade.

Courtelle keeps this skimmy shape—for ever!

1970s

Clothes with an ethnic, natural and 'rootsy' feel dominated the first few years of the 1970s as people explored New Age thinking and cheaper air travel made it possible to visit far-flung places. The hippy fashions from the previous decade were reworked with a folksy vibe, taking traditional crafts such as knitting, tapestry, weaving and dyeing to the very epicentre of fashion. The Art Deco revival, triggered by the work of Royal College of Art lecturer Bernard Nevill for Liberty, flourished. Barbara Hulanicki's Biba store became a mecca for the vintage look. New inspiration was born through collaborations of fashion and art in the work of designers such as Ossie Clark and Celia Birtwell, and Bill Gibb and Zandra Rhodes. Malcolm McLaren sold 1950s memorabilia at his Let It Rock shop before pulling the plug on the whole retro trend in 1974 and opening a new shop called simply SEX. In 1977 he and partner Vivienne Westwood renamed their shop Seditionaries while simultaneously launching the pop career of the Sex Pistols. Meanwhile, ready-to-wear fashion established a solid base, with Givenchy, Oscar de la Renta, Yves Saint Laurent, Marc Bohan for Dior and Karl Lagerfeld for Chloé wholesaleing around the world. Inspired by the groundbreaking work of British designer Jean Muir and Saint Laurent, Calvin Klein, Geoffrey Beene, Ralph Lauren and others created new, flowing jersey separates and easy-to-wear classics for working women. Diane von Furstenberg's signature wraparound dress was a huge hit and New York's Studio 54 became the most famous discotheque in the world.

Bodystockings

A one-piece close-fitting garment made of elastic material and enveloping the whole body like a leotard. Originally worn by dancers, it became popular during the disco craze and was part of the slinky look of fluid 1970s fabrics that also harked back to 1930s Hollywood glamour.

Maxi skirts

The ankle- or floor-length skirt was a counter to the 1960s miniskirt (considered politically incorrect by many 1970s feminists). In dress form the maxi was often worn with a choker and crochet shawl and had an A-line skirt with a fitted bodice.

Wraparound

Diane von Furstenberg's signature wrap dress was a classic that spawned wraparound skirts and tops for the mass market. Her simple knit jersey wrap launched in 1972.

Diana décolleté

An asymmetric neckline with one bare shoulder, first seen in the second half of the nineteenth century and adopted by Elsa Schiaparelli in the 1930s, and Madame Grès in the 1950s, it regained popularity in the late 1970s, especially under the development of Roy Halston.

Parkas

A comfortable, lined, long outer garment with large pockets, usually made of tough cotton fabric with a removable lining; initially designed as an all-weather jacket for soldiers. It became very popular with young people in the 1970s.

Key looks of the decade

1970s

Jumpsuits

One-piece 'Charlie's Angels' pantsuit, usually with short legs made of elastic material, such as jersey. Along with this trend came tube dresses, with a reduced figure-hugging outline in plain colours of white, beige or pastels.

▼Unisex

In the 1970s Rudi Gernreich explored unisex fashion, which he carried to an extreme by using identical clothing on totally hairless male and female models. The androgynous look of Diane Keaton in *Annie Hall,* as below, and musician Patti Smith were part of the trend.

Carmen and gipsy looks

A flamenco style and part of the ethnic fashion of the decade. The look was modelled on Spanish flamenco costume, usually narrow at the hips, thighs and knees and ending in a wide skirt, with lace or frills at the off-the-shoulder neckline. Similarly, the gipsy look was characterized by frilled or unevenly hemmed skirts worn with blouses tied above the waist.

Gauchos, knickerbockers and jodhpurs

Mid-length trousers included the calf-length wide-bottomed gauchos, based on South American cowboys; full breeches gathered below the knee; and traditional riding breeches, very full from hip to knee, narrow on the calves and usually with a leather insert on the inside leg.

▲Kaftans

Along with kimonos, muumuus, djellaba (a Moroccan hooded robe) or jalabiya (a loose eastern robe) and other styles from India and Africa, kaftans were translated into westernized loungewear. They were especially suited as eveningwear when designed in exotic fabrics and edged in metallic trims, as this one in gold thread for Pierre Cardin, 1973.

olkloric

ry type of ethnic image set
end. A peasant fashion for
lets with lacing, braid trim
false bibbed blouses became
versal. The ethnic influence,
seen in this 1970 Zandra
odes piece, was so strong
it revived craft skills from
flung places, seen in Tibetan
Chinese quilted jackets,
are armhole waistcoats,
chworking and macramé.

Flares and trousersuits

Trousers and 'pantsuits' were
serious fashions in the 1970s.
They began gently flared then
reached wide bell-bottom
proportions by about 1975, after
which they slowly reduced to
straight and wide until, by the end
of the decade, they were finally
narrow again. Popular fabrics
included heavy crepes, wool jersey
knits, Courtelle jersey and woven
polyester suiting such as Trevira.

Patterns, prints and colours

An abundance of floral motifs
and nature patterns emerged,
although geometrics and stripes
continued from the 1960s, albeit
in prints and patterns (such as
in African and Native American
textiles) rather than in form and
cut. Typified by a sober neutral
palette of white, black, beiges and
olives, earth tones were the mark
of the day, set off by mustard,
brick red and dark orange.

Eastern influences

Kenzo, Yuki and Zoran were all
1970s labels that developed from
an eastern minimalist point. As
epitomized by Rei Kawakubo
and Comme des Garçons, along
with Issey Miyake and Yohji
Yamomoto, the movement
produced clothes that were
refined, fluid and sculptural. In
Kawakubo's case this included
ruching and asymmetry.

Hotpants

ming into fashion in the early
Os, these were extremely
ef shorts that barely covered
bottom, and appeared in
vet or lurex for eveningwear.
ey were often worn under a
toned maxi or midi skirt with
front opened to reveal lots of
. As is typical of synthetics of
period, these items are rarely
nd in good condition.

▲Granny dresses

Dresses with empire waistlines,
an ornate fabric bodice and
exotic sleeves were popular in
a feminine, Earth Mother way,
as was the granny dress with a
high frilled or lace neckline and
floral prints on brushed fabric.
Laura Ashley contributed to the
fashion with her romantic floral
cotton prints and deliberately
old-fashioned dresses reminiscent
of the Victorian era.

Punk

Led by Malcolm McLaren and
Vivienne Westwood, the punk
movement was deconstructive
and anti-establishment; it was
characterized by bondage, safety
pins, ripped edges and chaotic,
irregular stitching. By 1977 Zandra
Rhodes was using punk elements
– gold safety pins and chains to
connect and decorate uneven
hems and slashed holes edged
with gold thread.

▲Disco fashion

Strongly influenced by 1977's
Saturday Night Fever, disco was
characterized by shiny, metallic
and glittery materials such as
sequins, Lurex and Spandex. The
pieces, including bandeau tops
and stretch skirts, were often
adaptations of dancewear that
made its way into discos. Gold
lamé, leopardskin and white
clothes that glowed in UV
lights captured the disco era.

LEFT Front and back views
of a 1971 Ossie Clark–Celia
Birtwell coat with puffed
sleeves, pointed lapel and
Birtwell's famous Floating
Daisy print. With its tie-front
fastening, the coat was
made to be worn over a
coordinating dress in the
same colourway.

OPPOSITE An alternative
variation of the Floating
Daisy design in another
Clark-Birtwell coat, this time
featuring the floral print
alongside a grid design on
the bodice, rounded collar
and sleeves. The buttons
intersect the grid neatly
down the bodice.

Decorative Arts and Crafts Revivals

Organic farming and self-sufficiency thrived alongside a revival of interest in traditional handcrafts in the 1970s. Night classes in knitting, macramé, embroidery, weaving and pottery began to appear. Detail became a crucial element of fashion, emerging all the way through the decade in different ways, from handcrafted knitted, woven and embroidered fabrics through to patchwork and pleating mid-decade, followed by another appliqué revival at the end of the decade.

Several designers of the 1970s were noted for their interest in reviving traditional craftsmanship. In Britain, Laura Ashley's early designs were inspired by country crafts, and yokes, smocking, embroidery, brocade and lace details set her clothes apart from more mass-produced versions. They helped to supply a growing market for traditional and even Victorian-style clothes.

Bill Gibb used wool, reworking such traditional knits as Fair Isle and Arran into different patterns and weaves with new properties. He put knitted waistcoats over evening dresses and gave the whole concept of knitting a new image. Crochet, knobbly textures, beading and unusually small or large stitches came to characterize his work, as more designers followed his lead and began to work with knitted fabrics. Gibb also liked to take traditional Scottish woven fabrics, including tweed, and give them a new twist. One of his 1970 designs features a heavily patterned pigskin jacket worn over a knife-pleated, checked tweed skirt. Although Gibb teamed up with American knitwear designer Kaffe Fassett on several occasions in joint ventures, he was destined never to capitalize on his creativity owing to constant financial difficulties.

Knitted fabrics were not just craft-inspired, folksy and ethnic-looking. Since the 1960s, designers including Sonia Rykiel and Missoni had been fashioning garments from stretchy knits. By the early 1970s such looks were big fashion news at other major houses, including Krizia. Missoni's trademark zig-zag, finely striped, multicolour knits helped to establish it as Milan's biggest fashion company, planting the northern Italian city firmly on the fashion map. Meanwhile, British names like Jeff Banks and Daniel Hechter entered the market with stylish knitted tank tops and V-necked, deep-ribbed, cuff-sleeved sweaters. The tabard-style overtop – a wide-sleeved, long-lined tunic, often belted at the waist and worn over a turtleneck sweater – was big news in 1976. Further down the fashion chain, knitwear became popular on the high street, with cheaper brands producing sporty hotpants, vests, leggings and legwarmers in cheaper acrylic knits.

LEFT Missoni 1970s top and fringed overshirt. The exceptional colours and textures have made Missoni pieces highly collectible and as popular today as since their inception by sisters Tai and Rosita Missoni in 1953. Worldwide attention started in the late '60s, and the 1970s saw them producing dresses, coats, skirts and trousers as well as sweaters.

OPPOSITE The back view of a 1979 knitted coat by Kaffe Fassett, who was known for his rich many-coloured palette and geometric patterns. The muted colours and full sleeves, which draw on Renaissance and Eastern dress, show his influential creative skills. The colours and shape also recall the work of Missoni and Bill Gibb; indeed, his early collections were commissioned by both.

1980s

The 1980s was the decade of 'Hard Times'; not just a song by the Human League and a popular London nightclub, 'Hard Times' was a way of life for many. Money, as Mick Hucknall sang, was literally 'too tight to mention'. This was the dawning of the age of Thatcher and Reagan, and the working classes were feeling the pinch. Street fashion, born out of broke fashion students' imaginations and a few ingenious musicians, was adopted as the uniform of the trendy. Those who could afford upmarket designer fashion from names like Gianni Versace, Louis Féraud, Claude Montana or Chanel were wealthy, but not fêted for their sense of style. Until clever designers like Jean Paul Gaultier picked up on street accents and adapted them, designer clothing remained a separate entity.

By the middle of the decade, things were looking up. The financial capitals of the world witnessed a boom and there was a sudden surge of interest in designer shoes, bags and jewellery – it was the birth of the label. New York became a fashion mecca. Calvin Klein, Donna Karan and Ralph Lauren were the big names, while on another level, hip-hop music began the passion for bling and sportswear tracksuits by Nike, Adidas and Reebok, teamed with gold chains, medallions, rings and the latest training shoes, became street fashion's most enduring look.

Nightclubbing was big news on both sides of the Atlantic and fashion was strongly influenced by the latest club looks. Stephen Sprouse and Norma Kamali dressed New York's clubbers, while individual designers including Antony Price and John Richmond with Maria Cornejo made names for themselves on London dance floors. Young, single heiresses, including Francesca Thyssen in London and Cornelia Guest in New York, dominated the people pages of style magazines like Andy Warhol's *Interview* in New York and Lord Lichfield's *Ritz* in London.

Androgyny

Style setters who included Annie Lennox and Grace Jones made the androgynous look big news with men's suits, ties and close-cropped hair, combined with the ultimate feminine touch – red lips or a corset-style basque.

▶ Streetwear

Letters, numbers and graphics made the oversize T-shirt the most popular single item in the 1980s. New York artist Keith Haring, his work shown here in a design for Vivienne Westwood, created simple graphic drawings that popped up everywhere.

Full skirts and layering

Vivienne Westwood's multilayered full skirts and sweaters worn with bras over the top, completed with chunky boots, epitomized the street urchin look.

White prairie skirts

Pioneers and prairie girls at Ralph Lauren and English roses at Laura Ashley wore white lace and broderie anglaise skirts and dresses. Full tiered skirts with peasant tops, accessorized with brown leather belts and purses, finished the look.

Key looks of the decade

1980s

▲ Stripes and tartan

Colour was riotous; Betty Jackson and Wendy Dagworthy sent models down runways in bulky, multicoloured tweeds. Short kilts and other traditional clothing returned, albeit in subverted styling.

Wide cinch belts

The cinched-in waist was the keypoint of 1980s dressing. A curvaceous silhouette came back into style with belts making a huge impact.

▶Suits and shoulders

The television programme *Dynasty* helped the power suit catch on worldwide, but couture had led the way: black-and-white dogstooth pencil skirts with a nipped-in jackets by Marc Bohan for Christian Dior and Giorgio Armani's 'Donna' ad campaign from 1984-85 were notable. Here a black-and-white 1983 Jean-Louis Scherrer suit exhibits the extreme styling of the silhouette.

...ersized

...sized looks featured in ...y catwalk collections, from ...arine Hamnett to Issey ...ke to Kenzo. This oversized ...dress, based on a man's work ..., but with deep side splits, ...rn with an oversized black ...er belt.

Puffball skirts

Christian Lacroix brought this little gem into style in 1986, hot on the heels of Vivienne Westwood's 'mini-crini'.

...mmetrics

...hed shoulders and halfway ...s, one-sleeve wonders and ...k Lycra with cut-outs were ...alent. Couture versions ...ded Comme des Garçons ...gns, especially as they ...ared on Kim Basinger in ...ilm *9 1/2 Weeks* (1986).

◀Laura Ashley dresses

Reaching its apogee in the early 1980s, Laura Ashley brought a sweet femininity to women's dresses that worked as a counter to the power suit, as shown left. The clothes had a neo-Victorian, old world romanticism that seemed to find relevance in the conservative tastes of the time.

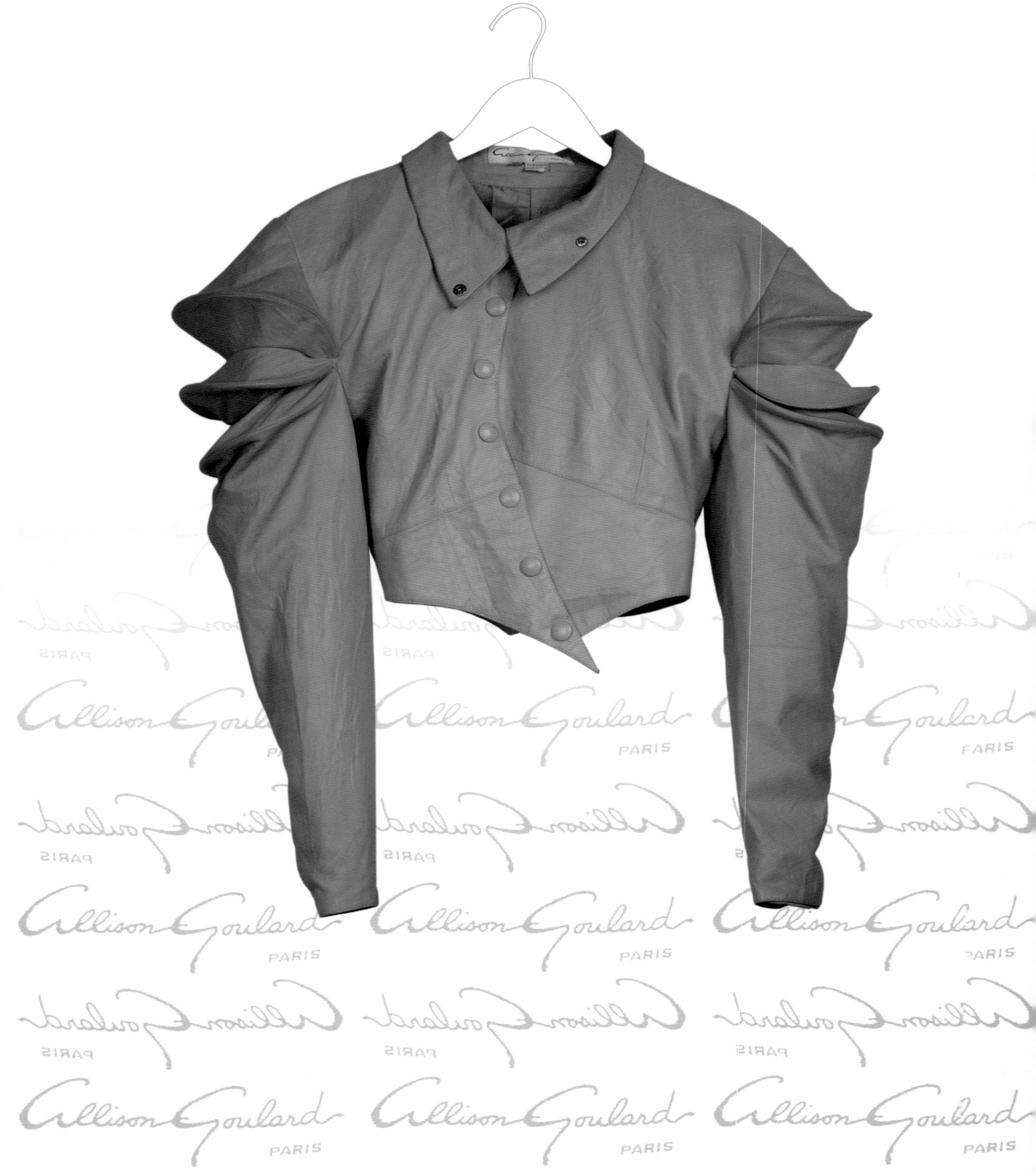
Allison Goulard
PARIS

OPPOSITE Light blue 1980s leather jacket, by American designer Allison Goulard. Note the built-up, conical spirals in the sleeve, classic 1980s oversized rounded shoulders, tapered cuffs and asymmetric hem. The jacket is likely to have been worn with high-waisted black ski-pants or a matching straight-cut leather mini.

ABOVE Jean-Paul Gaultier 1980s animal-print jacket. His clothes have a kind of kitschy glamour that made them popular show-off items. He used details such as metal tips on collars and his jackets were highly structured and fitted to exaggerate the female body.

Shopping Guide by Mark and Cleo Butterfield

Most people who collect and wear designer fashions do so simply because of the sheer pleasure involved. The hunt for a good piece, the knowledge you gain in the process and the personal stories you hear along the way can be as compelling as finding and purchasing a highly desired, sought-after piece. Whether your aim is collecting a specific designer or within a particular time period, or finding a unique piece you know no one else will have or wear, there are a few ground rules and tips to keep in mind, which will help you locate the best pieces for you.

First of all, know what you are buying. There really is no substitute for the experience gained from seeing and handling vintage pieces.

Where to buy

Specialist vintage fashion fairs and markets are a great opportunity to meet a lot of dealers and see a huge variety of classic vintage clothing gathered together in one place. Specialist shops and viewings at major auction houses are also excellent places to see a high concentration of quality pieces. Here you can familiarize yourself with clothes from different periods and the work of specific designers.

Online auctions such as eBay can be full of pitfalls for the unwary. First, the seller is unlikely to be a vintage dealer and may know very little about the garment they are auctioning. Without any deliberate attempt to mislead, items are quite frequently incorrectly assigned to periods or accredited to designers. Second, there's no way of seeing the item to check its condition. Always email the seller about stains, repairs, alterations, etc, and ask to see the label if it hasn't been shown.

Buying tips

- ❖ Never buy a stained garment with the hope that it will come out with washing or dry cleaning. If the mark's been there for a long time, it probably isn't going to shift. Get a full description of stains, such as rust, mildew or sweat, as well as any odours.
- ❖ Always check the item thoroughly for condition. Hold it up to the light to reveal any moth holes. Check both sides of the fabric for scorches, tears, mended areas, missing beadwork or embellishments and for disintegration of any type. Any professional seller will automatically point out tears or other signs of damage, but always ask.
- ❖ Focus on a particular time period or designer; you will gain deeper knowledge about a specialized subject and meet like-minded buyers and sellers who will further your experience and be able to give you

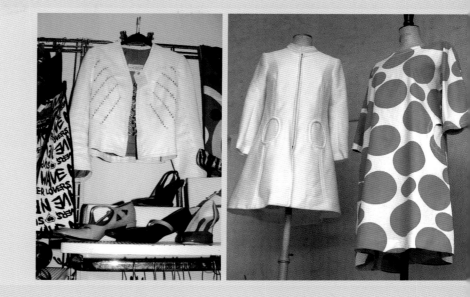

'Fashion is not something that exists in dresses only… fashion has to do with ideas, the way we live, what is happening.'
Coco Chanel

more information on the subject. This will also help you focus on your aim, rather than trying to pick from what you like of a century's worth of designs.

❖ If you are buying for a collection or investment, look for pieces that typify a designer's work and always buy the best pieces that you can afford.

❖ If you are buying for wearing the clothes, follow the sizing tips on page 210 so that you choose the era that best suits your body shape and inherent style; otherwise you may feel uncomfortable, or as if you are wearing a costume rather than a piece that makes you look and feel great.

❖ Couture dresses claim the highest prices, but the price also depends on the designer, age, workmanship, condition and size; if you are keen for a specific designer, for example, you may compromise on size or condition to own it. Likewise you may accept an unauthenticated piece if the detailing is remarkably rare or beautiful.

❖ Many sellers use standard descriptions to indicate the condition of the garment: **mint** is rare and perfect, probably never worn; **near mint** indicates light wear, as in evening dresses; **excellent** means it is sound with some wear but no flaws; **very good** indicates minor flaws or stains but otherwise high quality; **good** means that it is wearable but shows some deterioration.

Dating garments

Once you have some experience handling period garments, you will develop an intrinsic sense of the time period. A knowledge of the fabrics, haberdashery and stitching techniques typical of the time will also give you good indications of the era. Familiarize yourself with fabric and trimming terms from past eras, and learn the difference between them and when they were in common use. The glossary on pages 217-19 will help, as well as the further reading on page 223. Construction methods and the silhouette of the garment are also good indicators – for example, garments were much more fitted before 1960. The underlying structure of the piece will also offer clues on whether the piece is couture or ready-to-wear, in the case of missing labels, and the value and age of the piece.

If the designer or label is known, this may help you identify the date by the time period the designer was active. Many designers changed the style of their name or label over time, or were affiliated with various brands – see pages 214-16 for the glossary, which lists the labels designers worked under.

When attempting to date garments, here are a few additional guidelines to help you pinpoint the date.

❖ Washing care labels only came into popular use in the 1970s.

*'The truly fashionable
are beyond fashion.'*
Cecil Beaton

❖ Zips were in use in the 1920s for heavy-duty fastenings, boots, and so on, but are not common in dresses until the postwar period. You will find some 1930s dresses with zips, but these were stopped during wartime because of utility restrictions.

❖ Plastic zips were introduced in the 1930s, but constructed along the same lines as metal zips, with individual teeth.

❖ Zips usually appeared in sides seams up until the 1950s, and later appeared in the centre back of dresses and skirts and the centre front of trousers.

❖ Most pre-war clothes were dressmaker-made and won't have labels.

❖ Machine overlocking of seams became widespread in the 1960s, so this can help you tell a modern copy from an original.

Sizes

As most clothing up to the 1960s was home- or dressmaker-made, there will be no size labels in pieces before this period. Each piece was bespoke, made for a specific person's shape, so for that dress to fit you perfectly you also have to be that same size. Standardization of sizes only came in with mass production. A 1960s or 1970s size would be expected to be one or two sizes smaller than a modern one, but waist measurements were proportionately smaller, so make sure you can try it on, or get all the measurements.

Thanks to better nutrition and exercise habits, however, women today are taller and bigger than ever before, so there's no substitute for trying the item on. If this isn't possible, ask for the seller to provide exact measurements, not only including length, waist and bust measurements but also the hip, cuff, sleeve length, neck opening, from nape to waist, back shoulder to shoulder, waist to hem, shoulder to hem, the circumference of the hemline, and any potentially restrictive areas, like under the upper arm.

In general, 1920s fashions generally suit the small and slight of figure; 1950s clothes are created along the hourglass line so they fit the curvaceous, though waists are very small; 1960s fashions are best on the tall and leggy.

Couture items

Many couture pieces are works of art, highly hand-constructed or hand-embellished and made of the finest materials available at the time. Authenticating a couture item can be very difficult; often the lining of a garment would wear through and be cut away, and along with it the label. Additionally, the best pieces are those made to measure, as a great deal of labour and craftsmanship went into the pieces; the name of the individual client often appears on the dress label.

Because these items will never be created again, and the level of artistry involved can never be repeated

due to cost and expertise limitations, couture items are highly covetable. Pieces showing exquisite handworked beading or embroidery, unique hand-dyed colours, luxury fabrics or unique techniques, such as Fortuny pleating, are especially desirable. Keep these, and the below tips, in mind when looking for couture.

❖ Labels with the designers name, an ink number and the client's name.

❖ Stitching that is fine, neat and even.

❖ The garment is likely to have been well cared for, so should be in good condition.

❖ Careful sewing of buttons, buttonholes, hooks and other closures, and fabric-covered or concealed fasteners.

❖ Lining and interior structure that is as well-crafted as the exterior.

Care and storage

If you are ever in doubt about whether a piece should be washed, consult a professional conservator or ask a costume dealer for advice, especially if you suspect the piece may be rare or you are unsure of the fragility of its materials. Do not ever use a washing machine or dryer for vintage pieces, and think carefully about pressing any item as it can press stains into the fabric. Steaming is usually a good option for robust fabrics.

There is a risk that moth, carpet beetle or their eggs could be lurking in the fibres of your latest vintage purchase and they will happily destroy the rest of your wardrobe. Wrap the piece in acid-free tissue paper, place it in a sealed plastic bag and put it in the freezer for three days. Be gentle when removing it, especially with silk items, and allow it gradually to defrost. Here are a few general tips you can follow.

❖ Always clean any new item before storing. If the garment has a cleaning label that says it can be washed, it is always safer to hand wash. If it there is no label and you think that it ought to be washable (for example, if it's made of cotton), test an inconspicuous part first.

❖ Modern washing powders may be too harsh and cause colours to run, so use a pure soap powder such as Lux.

❖ Never wash a 1920s sequin dress, as the sequins are made of gelatine, and will dissolve in the water!

❖ Many older fabrics are not colour-fast and may discolour, shrink or distort, particularly any that are based on silk, acetate or rayon.

❖ Consider not only the fabric of the piece, but also any trims or linings.

❖ Dry cleaning is damaging to many fabrics, and may require the removal of labels or accessories, which will devalue the piece.

❖ Don't store anything in plastic. Natural fibres will hold moisture and once housed in the mini greenhouse of a plastic cover will release the water which may mark your garment. Wrap it in acid-free tissue and keep it in a cardboard box.

Collections & Stores

Museums & Collections

UNITED KINGDOM

Design Museum
Shad Thames
London SE1 2YD
Tel: 0870 833 9955
Email: info@designmuseum.org
Website: www.designmuseum.org
A showcase for all design genres,
including fashion.

The Fashion and Textile Museum
88 Bermondsey Street
London SE1 3XF
Tel: 020 7403 0222
Email: info@ftmlondon.org
Website: www.ftmlondon.org
Opened by Zandra Rhodes. Shows the
best of vintage and modern fashion
and textiles, with rotating exhibitions
featuring such designers as Vivienne
Westwood and Ossie Clark.

Gallery of Costume
Platt Hall, Rusholme
Manchester M14 5LL
Tel: 0161 224 5217
www.manchestergalleries.org
One of Britain's largest collections of clothing
and accessories, dating from the seventeenth
century to the present day.

Museum of Costume
Bennett Street
Bath BA1 2QH
Tel: 01225 477173
Email: costume_enquiries@bathnes.gov.uk
Website: http://www.museumofcostume.co.uk
Eveningwear from the 1900s to the 1950s,
as well as iconic 1960s and 1970s designs.
Annual exhibitions highlighting
a particular aspect of fashion.

Victoria and Albert Museum
Cromwell Road
London SW7 2RL
Tel: 020 7942 2000
Email: textilesandfashion@vam.ac.uk
Website: http://www.vam.ac.uk
Fashion and textile collection dating
from the seventeenth century to the
present day, with an emphasis on
influential European design. Also
showcases accessories such as gloves,
jewellery and handbags.

UNITED STATES

Cornell Costume and Textile Collection
Department of Textiles and Apparel
Cornell University
Ithaca, NY 14853-4401
Tel: 607 255 2235
Email: caj7@cornell.edu
Website (curator): www.human.cornell.edu
Website (online gallery):
costume.cornell.edu/greetingdb.htm
Cornell Costume and Textile Collection of
more than 9,000 items, a selection of which
are on public display during normal weekday
hours when the university is in session.
Online gallery also available.

The Costume Institute
The Metropolitan Museum of Art
1000 Fifth Avenue at 82nd Street
New York, NY 10028-0198
Tel: 212 535 7710
Email: thecostumeinstitute@metmuseum.org
Website: www.metmuseum.org
Vast collection of 80,000 costumes.

Hope B McCormick Costume Center
Clark Street at North Avenue
Chicago, IL 60614-6071
Tel: 312 642-4600
Webmail: www.chicagohs.org
A collection of 50,000 pieces, including
historical costumes and designer items by
such names as Charles Worth, Paul Poiret
and Issey Miyake.

The Kent State University Museum
PO Box 5190
Rockwell Hall
Kent, OH 44242-0001
Tel: 330 672 3450
Email: museum@kent.edu
Website: www.kent.edu/museum
A collection of mainly twentieth-century
garments, representing the work of most
major American and European designers,
including some of their archives and sketch-
books. Stages exhibitions from its collection.

Vintage Fashion Museum
212 N. Broadway
Abilene, KS 67410
Tel: 785 263 7997
Email: fashion@ikansas.com
Website: www.abilenekansas.org
Fashions from the 1870s to the 1970s.

CANADA

Costume Museum of Canada
Box 38
Dugald, Manitoba
Tel: 204 8532166
Freephone: 1866 853 2166
Email: info@costumemuseum.com
Website: costumemuseum.com
Intended as a national repository for
costume, textiles and accessories, the
collection includes designs by Chanel,
Norman Hartnell, Worth, Schiaparelli,
Vionnet, Scassi and Paco Rabanne.

AUSTRALIA

Powerhouse Museum
500 Harris Street Ultimo
PO Box K346
Haymarket, Sydney
New South Wales 1238
Tel: 61 2 9217 0111
Website: www.powerhousemuseum.com
Occasional exhibitions of contemporary
and vintage fashion and style icons, such
as Audrey Hepburn.

Stores and Boutiques

UNITED KINGDOM

Appleby
95 Westbourne Park Villas
London W2 5ED
Tel: 020 7229 7772
Email: jane@applebyvintage.com
Website: www.applebyvintage.com
Friendly and accommodating vintage
boutique run by Jane Appleby.

Blackout II
51 Endell Street
London WC2 9HJ
Tel: 020 7240 5006
Email: clothes@blackout2.com
Website: www.blackout2.com
Specializes in clothing from the 1930s
and 1940s.

Cenci
4 Nettlefold Place
London SE27 0JW
Tel: 020 8766 8564
Email: info@cenci.co.uk
Website: www.cenci.co.uk
Vintage fashion and accessories from
the 1930s onwards.

C20 Vintage Fashion
Email: enquiries@c20vintagefashion.co.uk
Website: www.c20vintagefashion.co.uk
Cleo and Mark Butterfield's inspirational
vintage garments are available for hire.

Decades
17-18 Dover Street
London W1S 4LT
Tel: 020 7518 0680
Email: info@decadesinc.com
Website: www.decadesinc.com

One of a Kind
253 Portobello Road
London W11 1LR
Tel: 020 7792 5284

Palette London
21 Canonbury Lane
London N1 2AS
Eclectic selection of vintage clothing.
Also a finder service.

Pop Boutique
6 Monmouth Street
London WC2H 9HB
Tel: 020 7497 5262
Email: info@pop-boutique.com
Website: www.madaboutpop.com
1960s, 1970s and 1980s originals as well
as its own retro Pop label.

Rellik
8 Golborne Road
London W10 5NW
Tel: 020 8962 0089
Website: www.relliklondon.co.uk
Clothing and accessories from the
1920s to mid-1980s.

Rokit
42 Shelton Street
Covent Garden
London WC2H 9HZ
Tel: 020 7836 6547
Website: www.rokit.co.uk

Steinberg & Tolkien
193 King's Road
London SW3 5ED
Tel: 020 7376 3660
Well-established shop owned by
Tracy Tolkien selling vintage clothing,
accessories and jewellery.

The Vintage Clothing Company
Afflecks Palace
Oldham Street
Manchester M4 1PW
Tel: 0161 832 0548
Website: www.vintageclothingcompany.com
Part of a chain of five retail outlets.

Virginia
98 Portland Road
London W11 4LQ
Tel: 020 7727 9908
Exquisite antique clothing.

UNITED STATES
Decades
8214 ½ Melrose Avenue
Los Angeles CA 90046
Tel: 323 655 0223
Website: www.decadesinc.com
Fabulous collection by Cameron Silver, who
has now opened his second shop in London.

Keni Valenti Retro-Couture
155 West 29th Street
Third floor, Room C5
New York, NY 10001
Tel: 212 967 7147
Website: www.kenivalenti.com

The Paper Bag Princess
8818 Olympic Boulevard
Beverly Hills CA 90211
Tel: 310 385 9036
Website: www.thepaperbagprincess.com

William Doyle Galleries
175 East 87th Street
New York, NY 10128
Tel: 212 427 2730
Email: info@DoyleNewYork.com
Website: www.doylegalleries.com
Auctioneers and appraisers of
haute couture and antique costume.

CANADA
Deluxe Junk Company
310 W Cordova Street
Vancouver, British Columbia V6B 1E8
Tel: 604 685-4871
Email: dlxjunk@telus.net
Website: www.deluxejunk.com
Vancouver's oldest vintage clothing store.
Great selection of vintage and contemporary
clothing, accessories and costume jewellery.

MaryAnn Harris
Ottawa Antique Market
1179 Bank Street
Ottawa, Ontario
Tel: 613 720 9242

AUSTRALIA
Vintage Clothing Shop
147-49 Castlereagh Street
Shop 5, CBD
Sydney 2000

Organizations

Vintage Fashion Guild
www.vintagefashionguild.org
An online resource set up by a collective
of vintage sellers. Offers information, news
and a virtual museum, plus guidance for
vintage vendors.

Costume Society
www.costumesociety.org.uk
The society includes collectors, curators,
designers, lecturers, students and informed
enthusiasts with the aim to explore all
aspects of clothing history.

Costume Society America
www.costumesocietyamerica.com
Dedicated to the history and conservation of
dress adornment and to interpreting culture
through appearance.

Online stores

www.antiquedress.com
www.antique-fashion.com
www.shockadelic.com
www.thefrock.com
www.tias.com/stores/decades
www.unique-vintage.com
www.vintageblues.com
www.vintagemartini.com
www.vintagetextile.com
www.vintagetrends.com
www.vintagevixen.com

Fashion websites

www.costumegallery.com
www.costumes.org
www.fabrics.net
www.fashionencyclopedia.com
www.fashion-era.com
www.pastpatterns.com
www.vpll.org

Glossary of Designers

Adolfo (1933-): Bergdorf Goodman; Emme; Adolfo

Adrian, Gilbert (1903-59): Paramount; Adrian Limited

Agnès, Madame (1910-40): Madame Agnès millinery

Alaïa, Azzedine (1940-): Christian Dior; Guy Laroche; Azzedine Alaïa

Amies, Sir Hardy (1909-2003): Lachasse; Hardy Amies

Armani, Giorgio (1934-): Nino Cerruti; Giorgio Armani

Ashley, Laura (1925-85): Laura Ashley

Augustabernard: founded by Augusta Bernard in 1919

Bakst, Léon (1866-1924): Ballets Russes

Balenciaga, Cristobal (1895-1972): Balenciaga couture house

Balmain, Pierre (1914-82): Robert Piguet; Edward Molyneux; Lucien Lelong; Balmain

Banton, Travis (1894-1958): Lucile Duff Gordon; Paramount; Twentieth-Century Fox; Universal Studios

Bates, John (1935-): Herbert Sidon; Jean Varon; John Bates

Beene, Geoffrey (1927-): Teal Traina; Geoffrey Beene Inc., Beenebag

Berardi, Antonio (1968-): Antonio Berardi

Biagiotti, Laura (1943-): Roberto Cappuci, Laura Biagiotti

Biba: Founded by Barbara Hulanicki (1936-) in 1964

Bikkembergs, Dirk (1962-): Freelance designer for Nero, Bassetti, Gruno and Chardin, Tiktiner, Gaffa, K, and Jaco Petti; Dirk Bikkembergs

Birtwell, Celia (1941-): Ossie Clark and others; Celia Birtwell, London

Blass, Bill (1922-2002): Anna Miller and Company; Maurice Retner; Bill Blass Limited

Bodymap: Founded by David Holah and Stevie Stewart in 1982

Bohan, Marc (1926-): Jean Patou; Robert Piguet; Edward Molyneux; Patou; Christian Dior; Hartnell

Boué Souers, House of: Founded by Jeanne Boué in 1899

Bruce, Liza (1955-): Liza Bruce

Burrows, Stephen (1943-): Stephen Burrows' World

Byblos: Founded in 1973

Cacharel, Jean (1932-): Jean Jourdan; Société Jean Cacharel

Callot Soeurs, House of: Founded by sisters Gerber, Bertrand and Chanterelle in 1895

Capucci, Roberto (1929-): Emilio Schuberth; Roberto Capucci

Cardin, Pierre (1922-): Madam Paquin; Elsa Schiaparelli; Christian Dior; Pierre Cardin

Carnegie, Hattie (1889-1956): Macy's; Hattie Carnegie Originals; Hattie Carnegie

Cashin, Bonnie (1915-2000): Adler and Adler; Twentieth-Century Fox; Bonnie Cashin Designs

Cassini, Oleg (1913-): Jean Patou; Edith Head; Oleg Cassini; Jacqueline Kennedy

Castelbajac Jean-Charles de (1949-): André Courrèges; Jean-Charles do Castelbajac

Cavanagh, John (1914-): Edward Molyneux; Pierre Balmain; John Cavanagh

Céline: Founded in 1973

Cerruti, Nino (1930-): Nino Cerruti

Chalayan, Hussein (1970-): Cartesia Ltd; Hussein Chalayan

Chanel, Gabrielle 'Coco' (1883-1971): House of Chanel

Chéruit, Madeleine: Founded by Madeleine Chéruit in 1900

Chloé: Founded by Gaby Aghion and Jacques Lanoir in 1952

Clark, Ossie (1942-96): Quorum; Radley; Evocative

Clergerie, Robert (1934-): Charles Jourdan; Clerma Company; J Fenestrier

Colonna, Jean (1955-): Balmain; Jean Colonna

Comme des Garçons: founded by Rei Kawakubo (1942-) in 1973

Connolly, Sybil (1921-98): Bradleys; Richard Alan; Sybil Connolly Inc.; Tiffany's

Courrèges, André (1923-): Jeanne Laufrie; Cristobal Balenciaga; André Courrèges

Crahay, Jules François (1917-88): Nina Ricci; Jeanne Lanvin

Creed, Charles Southey (1909-66): Linton Tweeds; Bergdorf Goodman; Charles Creed

Daché, Lilly (1907-89): Reboux; Macy's; The Bonnet Shop; Travis Banton

De la Renta, Oscar (1932-): Cristobal Balenciaga; Lanvin; Oscar de la Renta

De Lisi, Ben (1955-): Saks; Penelope; Benedetto; Ben de Lisi

De Prémonville, Myrène (1949-): Myrène de Prémonville

Delaunay, Sonia (1885-1979): abstract painter and designer.

Demeulemeester, Ann (1959-): Ann Demeulemeester

Dessès, Jean (1904-70): Jean Dessès; Jean Dessès American Collection

Dior, Christian (1905-57): Robert Piguet; Lelong; Maison Dior; House of Christian Dior

Doeuillet, House of: Founded by Georges Doeuillet in 1900

Dolce & Gabbana: Founded by Dominco Dolce and Stefano Gabbana in 1985

Doucet, Jacques (1853-1929): Maison Doucet

Duff Gordon, Lucille (1862-1935): Lucile couture house

Edelstein, Victor (1947-): Alexon; Biba; Christian Dior; Victor Edelstein

Elbaz, Alber (1961-): Geoffrey Beene; Guy Laroche; YSL Rive Gauche

Ellis, Perry (1940-86): Miller & Rhoads; Perry Ellis International

Emanuel, David (1952-) and Elizabeth (1953-): Emanuel

Erté (Romaine de Tirtoff 1892-1990): Costume designs for ballet and theatre

Estrada, Angel (1957-89): Estrada

Ettedgui, Joseph (1936-): Chain of shops including Joseph, Joseph Tricot, Joseph Pour La Maison

Fath, Jacques (1912-54): Jacques Fath couture house

Fendi: Founded by Adele Casagrande in 1918

Féraud, Louis (1921-99): Louis Féraud

Ferragamo, Salvatore (1898-1960): Bonito;
Salvatore Ferragamo

Ferre, Gianfranco (1944-): Gianfranco Ferre Donna;
Christian Dior; Gianfranco Ferre

Ferretti, Alberta (1950-): Aeffe

Fiorucci, Elio: Founded by Elio Fiorucci in 1962

Flett, John (1963-91): Lanvin; Enrico Coveri

Foale & Tuffin: Founded by Marion Foale and
Sally Tuffin in 1961

Ford, Tom (1962-): Cathy Harwick; Perry Ellis; Gucci;
YSL Rive Gauche

Fortuny, Mariano (1871-1949): Fortuny couture house

Fox, Frederick (1931-): Otto Lucas; Mitzi Lorenz; Langée;
Frederick Fox

Fratini, Gina (1934-): Katherine Dunham dance group;
Hartnell; Gina Fratini

Galanos, James (1924-): Hattie Carnegie; Piguet; Davidow;
Galanos Originals

Galliano, John (1960-) John Galliano; Givenchy; Christian Dior

Gaultier, Jean Paul (1952-): Pierre Cardin; Esterel; Jean Patou;
Jean Paul Gaultier SA

Gernreich, Rudi (1922-85): Lester Horton Dance Company;
William Bass; GR Designs; Rudi Gernreich Inc.

Gibb, Bill (1943-88): Baccarat; Bill Gibb Fashion Group

Gigli, Romeo (1949-): Dimitri Couture; Romeo Gigli

Givenchy, Hubert de (1927-): Jaques Fath; Robert Piguet;
Lucien Lelong; Elsa Schiaparelli; Maison Givenchy

Godley, Georgina (1955-): Crolla; Georgina Godley Ltd

Greer, Howard (1896-1974): Paul Poiret; Edward Molyneux;
Paramount; Howard Greer

Grès, Madame (1903-93): Premet; Alix

Griffe, Jacques (1917-): Vionnet; Edward Molyneux,
Jacques Griffe

Gucci, Guccio (1881-1953): Gucci

Halston, Roy Frowick (1932-90): Lilly Daché; Bergdorf Goodman;
Halston Ltd

Hamnett, Katharine (1948-): Tuttabanken Sportswear;
Katharine Hamnett Ltd

Hartnell, Sir Norman (1901-79): Madame Desirée;
Norman Hartnell

Head, Edith (1907-81): Paramount Studios; Universal Studios

Heim, Jacques (1899-1967): Jacques Heim

Hermès: Founded by Thierry Hermès in 1837

Howell, Margaret (1946-): Margaret Howell

Jackson, Betty (1949-): Quorum Design Studio; Betty Jackson

Jacobs, Marc (1964-): Ruben Thomas Inc.; Perry Ellis;
Marc Jacobs; Louis Vuitton

James, Charles (1906-78): E Haweis James; Charles James

Johnson, Betsey (1942-): Paraphernalia Boutiques; Betsey, Bunky
& Nini; Alvin Duskin Co.; Alley Cat; Betsey Johnson; BJ Vines

Jones, Stephen (1957-): Fiorucci; Stephen Jones

Kamali, Norma (1945-): Kamili; OMO Norma Kamali boutiques

Karan, Donna (1948-): Anne Klein; Donna Karan; DKNY

Kelly, Patrick (1954-90): Le Palais club; Patrick Kelly, Paris

Kenzo (1939-): Freelance designer to Féraud; Rodier; Pisanti;
Jungle Jap; Kenzo

Keogh, Lainey (1957-): Lainey Keogh

Kerrigan, Daryl (1964-): Daryl Kerrigan

Khanh, Emmanuelle (1937-): Cacharel; Dorothée Bis;
Emmanuelle Khanh

Klein, Anne (1923-74): Varden Petites; Anne Klein

Klein, Calvin (1942-): Dan Millstein; Calvin Klein Co.

Kors, Michael (1959-): Michael Kors; Céline

Krizia: founded by Mariuccia Mandelli in 1954

Lachasse, House of: Founded in 1928

Lacroix, Christian (1951-): Hermès; Guy Paulin; Jean Patou;
Christian Lacroix

Lagerfeld, Karl (1938-): Balmain; Patou; Chloé; Krizia; Chanel

Lang, Helmut (1956-): Helmut Lang

Lanvin, Jeanne (1867-1946): Jeanne Lanvin couture house

Lapidus, Ted (1929-): Ted Lapidus

Laroche, Guy (1923-89): Jean Dessès; Guy Laroche couture house

Lauren, Ralph (1939-): Polo Fashions; Polo Ralph Lauren

Léger, Hervé (1957-): Fendi; Chanel; Lanvin; Chloé;
Charles Jourdan; Hervé Léger

Lelong, Lucien (1889-1958): House of Lelong

Lesage: Founded by Albert Lesage in 1868

Lester, Charles & Patricia: Founded by Charles and Patricia
Lester in 1964

Liberty: Founded by Arthur Lasenby in 1875

Loewe: Founded by Enrique Loewe in 1846

Louiseboulanger: Founded by Louise Boulanger in 1927

Lucas, Otto (1903-71): Otto Lucas

McCardell, Claire (1905-58): Emmet Joyce; Robert Turk;
Townley Frocks; Hattie Carnegie

McFadden, Mary (1938-): Mary McFadden

Mackie, Bob (1940-): Cole of California, Bob Mackie Originals

Mainbocher (1890-1976): Mainbocher couture house

Margiela, Martin (1957-): Jean Paul Gaultier; Martin Margiela

Matsuda, Mitsuhiro (1934-): Nicole Limited; Matsuda

Maxmara: Founded by Achille Maramotti in 1951;
encompasses 16 labels

Missoni: Founded by Ottavio and Rosita Missoni in 1953

Miyake, Issey (1938-): Laroche; Givenchy; Geoffrey Beene;
Issey Miyake

Mizrahi, Isaac (1961-): Perry Ellis; Calvin Klein; Isaac Mizrahi

Model, Philippe (1956-): shoes and accessories – worked with Gaultier, Claude Montana, Issey Miyake and Thierry Mugler

Molinari, Anna (1948): Blumarine

Molyneux, Captain Edward (1891-1974): Lucile; Molyneux

Montana, Claude (1949-): Idéal-Cuir; MacDougal Leathers; Lanvin

Morton, Digby (1906-83): Digby Morton

Moschino, Franco (1950-94): Gianni Versace; Cadette; Moschino

Mugler, Thierry (1948-): Gudule boutique; André Peters; Thierry Mugler

Muir, Jean (1928-95): Jacqmar; Jaeger; Courtaulds; Jane & Jane; Jean Muir Ltd

Norell, Norman (1900-72): Brooks Costume Company; Charles Amour; Hattie Carnegie; Triana-Norell

Nutter, Tommy (1943-92): Donaldson, Williams & Ward; Tommy Nutter; Austin Reed

Oldfield, Bruce (1950-): Bruce Oldfield Ltd

Oldham, Todd (1961-): L-7; Todd Oldham

Orry-Kelly, John (1898-1964): costume design for Warner Brothers; Twentieth-Century Fox; Universal Studios; MGM

Ozbek, Rifat (1953-): Trell; Monsoon; Ozbek; Future Ozbek

Paquin: Founded by Jeanne Beckers and Isidore Jacobs in 1891

Patou, Jean (1880-1936): Jean Patou

Pertegaz, Manuel (1918-): Manuel Pertegaz

Piguet, Robert (1901-53): Paul Poiret; John Redfern; Robert Piguet

Plunkett, Walter (1902-82): RKO; MGM

Poiret, Paul (1879-1947): Charles Worth; Jacques Doucet; Paul Poiret

Porter, Thea (1927-2000): Thea Porter

Prada: Founded by Mario Prada in 1913

Price, Anthony (1945-): Stirling Cooper; Plaza; Antony Price

Pucci, Marchese Emilio (1914-92): Lord & Taylor; Pucci

Quant, Mary (1934-): Bazaar; Mary Quant Ginger Group

Rabanne, Paco (1934-): Givenchy; Dior; Balenciaga; Paco Rabanne

Reboux, Caroline (1830-1927): Vionnet; Caroline Reboux

Redfern: Founded by John Redfern in 1881

Rhodes, Zandra (1940-): Zandra Rhodes Ltd

Ricci, Nina (1883-1970): Nina Ricci couture house

Rocha, John (1953-): John Rocha

Rodriquez, Narciso (1961-): Calvin Klein; Cerruti; Loewe

Rouff, Maggy (1896-1971): Drécoll; Maggy Rouff

Rykiel, Sonia (1930-): Laura Boutique; Sonia Rykiel

Saint Laurent, Yves (1936-): Christian Dior; Yves Saint Laurent; YSL Rive Gauche

Sander, Jil (1943-): Jil Sander

Sant'Angelo, Giorgio di (1936-89): Sant'Angelo

Sassoon, Bellville: Founded by Belinda Bellville and David Sassoon in 1958

Scaasi, Arnold (1931-): Jeanne Paquin; Lilly Daché; Charles James; Arnold Scaasi

Scherrer, Jean-Louis (1936-): Christian Dior; Yves Saint Laurent; Louis Féraud; Jean-Louis Scherrer

Schiaparelli, Elsa (1890-1973): House of Schiaparelli – worked with Salvador Dalí, Christian Bérard and Jean Cocteau

Schön, Mila (1919-): Mila Schön

Sharaff, Irene (1910-93): Aline Bernstein; MGM

Sitbon, Martine (1951-): Chloé; Martine Sitbon

Sprouse, Stephen (1953-): Halston; Bill Blass; Stephen Sprouse

Stiebel, Victor (1907-76): Reville; Rossiter; Victor Stiebel; Jacqmar

Sui, Anna (1955-): Simultanee; Anna Sui

Tarlazzi, Angelo (1942-): Carosa; Patou; Angelo Tarlazzi; Guy Laroche

Thomass, Chantal (1947-): Dorothée Bis; Chantal Thomass

Trigère, Pauline (1912-2002): Hattie Carnegie; Pauline Trigère

Tyler, Richard (1946-): Anne Klein; Byblos; Richard Tyler Couture; Richard Tyler Collection

Ungaro, Emanuel (1933-): Cristobal Balanciaga; André Courrèges; Emanuel Ungaro couture house

Valentino (1932-): Jean Dessès; Guy Laroche; Valentino

Vanderbilt, Gloria (1924-): Gloria Vanderbilt

Van Noten, Dries (1958-): Dries Van Noten

Versace, Gianni (1946-97): Callaghan; Genny; Complice; Gianni Versace

Vionnet, Madeleine (1876-1975): House of Vincent; Kate Reilly; Callot Soeurs; Jacques Doucet; House of Vionnet

Vittadini, Adrienne (1944-): Louis Féraud; Sport Tempo; Warnaco; Kimberly Knits; Adrienne Vittadini

Von Furstenberg, Diane (1946-): Diane Von Furstenberg Studio; Diane Von Furstenberg couture house

Walker, Catherine (1945-): Chelsea Design Company

Watanabe, Junya (1961-): Rei Kawakubo

Westwood, Vivienne (1941-): Vivienne Westwood

Workers for Freedom: Founded by Richard Nott and Graham Fraser in 1985

Worth, Charles Frederick (1825-95): House of Worth

Yamamoto, Kansai (1944-): Junko Koshino; Hisashi Hosono; Yamamoto Kansai Company Ltd

Yamamoto, Yohji (1943-): Yohji Yamamoto

Yuki (1937-): Louis Féraud; Michael Donellan; Norman Hartnell; Pierre Cardin; Yuki

Zoran (1947-): Zoran

Glossary of Fashion Terms

Acetate: based on cellulose, this chemical fibre was first manufactured in 1864 and has been in mass production since 1920.

Ajouré: collective description of fine openwork, embroidered fabric.

A-line: created by Christian Dior, A-line describes a dress shaped in cutline like the letter A. From narrow shoulders and a low waist, it flares out to a wide skirt.

American shoulder: an armhole obliquely cut to reveal the shoulder.

Argyll (also Argyle): often seen on woollen socks and sweaters, this diamond pattern was named after an area of western Scotland.

Armani sleeves: turned-up sleeves created from two different fabrics.

Baker's check: similar in pattern to gingham, but twice the size.

Ballerina length: hem length of a dress or skirt that falls just above the ankles.

Balloon skirt: wide skirt hemmed to curve inward at the knees. Fashionable in cocktail dresses until 1958; enjoyed a revival in the late 1980s and again as part of the late 1990s retro look.

Balloon sleeve: created in 1890, this very full sleeve is held in place by a cuff at the wrist. Later revived by Nina Ricci.

Bateâu sleeve: also known as a boat neck, this is a collarless, boat-shaped neckline that runs from shoulder to shoulder.

Batwing sleeve: set deep and wide in the armhole, this sleeve tapers toward a tight wrist.

Besom pocket: a pocket sewn inside the garment with a slit welt opening.

Bias cut: a technique of cutting across the grain of the fabric, introduced in the 1920s by Madeleine Vionnet.

Blouson: popular in the 1950s, a hip-length sports jacket with a drawstring around the base, which gathers at the hips.

Body stocking: close-fitting, one-piece garment of elastic material and covering the whole body.

Bolero: open, waist-length jacket adopted from Spanish national costume.

Bomber jacket: military-style, blouson jacket, usually made of nylon.

Bord-à-bord jacket: women's jacket in which the front edges abut rather than cross. Held together with toggles or frogs, etc.

Boule shape: similar to Paul Poiret's hobble skirt, this is a skirt that is full below the waist, becoming tighter at the hem.

Box skirt: a straight skirt with a waistband and two thick, often quilted monk's seams running along the front and back.

Bustier: corset-like, strapless top of variable length above the waist. First worn as an undergarment, corsets are now worn as outerwear.

Bustle: pad or hoops used as a base over which the rear of a skirt is draped to emphasize the derrière. First in fashion around 1785, it was later adapted by Christian Dior and more recently by Vivienne Westwood.

Camel hair: soft, short undercoat of the camel from which a soft, woollen fabric is made.

Capri pants: narrow, three-quarter length ladies' trousers with a small slit at the side of the hem. Created by Emilio Pucci in the 1950s, Capri pants were inspired by trousers worn by Italian fishermen.

Casaque: fashionable in the 1920s, 1930s and 1950s, this hip-length blouse is worn over a skirt or as a pinafore over trousers around 1965-70.

Cascade neckline: this neckline consists of narrow straps and a cascade of fabric at the front.

Cashmere: the hair of the Kashmir goat is used to make a soft, light wool.

Cauterization: acid is applied to a blended fabric to destroy part of one of the types of fibre and creates a pattern – for example, devoré velvet.

Chalk stripes: pale stripes set on a dark background but less defined and spaced wider apart than pin stripes.

Chantilly lace: fine black bobbin lace, often with Baroque or Rococo style motifs or swags of flowers.

Chasuble pleat: a pleat covering the top seams of sleeves, it broadens the appearance of the shoulders.

Chauffe-coeur: sleeve vest created from warm fabric with a low-cut, round neck. Barely waist-length, it was adapted from ballet clothes.

Chenille: cut in the warp of a fabric, the fibres of this yarn stand proud and produce a similar effect to velvet. Chenille yarn is used to make corduroy and velour; also towelling and carpets.

Chiffon: translucent, light fabric with an uneven surface and made from synthetic fibres or natural silk.

Circular skirt: based on a circular or semicircular cut, this skirt is narrow at the hips and frequently supported by godets.

Cocktail dress: a short dress, often with a low neckline. Suitable for a variety of occasions when worn with a bolero or short jacket, this dress dates back to the 1940s.

Colour blocking: contrasting expanses of colour on fabric give clothes a graphic quality, as in Courrèges designs.

Corsair pants: narrow trousers cut slightly wider than Capri pants with slits below the knees.

Cossack pants: ankle- or calf-length trousers, baggy with a wide waist held by a belt.

Cowl neck: this wide piece of fabric tubing is attached to the neck of a garment.

Crepe: heat and a crêpe weave give this fabric its wrinkled surface.

Crepe de chine: made from natural or synthetic silk, this is a delicate, sheer and crinkled fabric.

Crinoline: originally made of horsehair and later steel hoops, this rigid petticoat gave width to skirts. Reappeared in Vivienne Westwood's mini crinis in 1980s.

Cup collar: open at the front, this stand-up collar is set at the back so the fabric falls in cup-like arches.

Cutouts: can area cut out of dresses, trousers and tops.

Diana décolleté: first seen in the second half of the nineteenth century, this asymmetric neckline featured one bare shoulder. In the 1930s it was adopted by Elsa Schiaparelli and then later on by Madam Grès in the 1950s. It regained popularity in the late 1970s.

Dior vent or Dior pleat: a short vent created for Christian Dior's 1948 tight pencil skirt.

Dirndl: this full skirt is gathered into the waistband.

Dolman sleeve: cut as an extension of the bodice, this sleeve was probably copied from the Turkish dolman. Emanuel Ungaro created an angular version, known as the Ungaro dolman, in 1968.

Empire line: dresses and coats are gathered beneath the bust and fall loosely to the feet. This style frequently comes back in fashion.

Encrustment: fabric pieces, such as leather, lace or trimmings, inserted into another yet distinct from appliqué.

Epaulet: originally designed to prevent slippage of shoulder-slung rifles and later a symbol of rank, this shoulderpiece gives a military touch to clothes. It first appeared in 1930s female fashions.

Flapper dress: fashionable in the 1920s, this dress featured narrow shoulder straps and a low waist, often tied with a scarf or belt.

Folkloric: dress style that assimilates elements of national costumes from around the world.

French cuffs: double cuffs.

French pocket: a pocket set in the side seams of a skirt or trousers.

Garçonne: severe, masculine style of dress of the 1920s.

Gaucho pants: wide-bottomed, calf-length trousers based on those worn by South American cowboys (gauchos); fashionable in the early 1970s.

Georgette crepe: translucent crêpe fabric

Gigot or leg-of-mutton sleeve: tight-fitting from cuffed wrist to elbow, this sleeve puffs up from elbow to shoulder.

Godet: sewn into a skirt, this triangular piece of fabric is designed to produce fullness.

Greatcoat reverse: named after the lapel on the greatcoat, which is produced by undoing the top button, this is a wide lapel.

Halterneck: top or dress with straps tied at the nape of the neck to leave the back and shoulders exposed.

Herringbone: produced by a broken twill weave and often emphasized with yarns in a variety of colours, this diagonally lined pattern resembles the skeleton of a herring.

H-line: launched by Christian Dior in 1954–55, this slightly tailored line has a slender top and narrow hips.

Hobble skirt: created by Paul Poiret in 1910, this ankle-length skirt is cut and draped to narrow beneath the knee, allowing only small steps to be taken.

Houndstooth: traditional small check pattern of two colours, often black and white. Due to the pattern linking individual checks, it is distinguishable from pepita (*see below*).

I-line: a narrow line silhouette created by Cristobal Balenciaga in 1954-55.

Jabot: used to cover buttons on dresses or blouses, this decorative frill became popular with women from the late nineteenth century until the late 1950s, and then became fashionable once more in a modified form in 1980.

Jersey: a generic term for different types of knitwear, jersey is a fabric that feels soft to the touch and is pliable without losing its shape; first introduced in haute couture by Coco Chanel in 1916-17.

Jodhpurs: riding breeches that are narrow on the calves and very full from hip to knee. Since the 1970s they have enjoyed various revivals.

Jumpsuit: one-piece trouser-suit usually made of an elastic material such as jersey and with short legs. Introduced in 1969.

Kaftan: loosely cut, straight and buttoned dress.

Kangaroo pocket: often seen on the front of cagoules, this is a large patch pocket.

Kimono sleeve: like the Japanese kimono, this is a straight sleeve that is secured at right angles to a garment.

Knickerbockers: loose, full breeches gathered beneath the knee, but more narrow than plus fours; revived in the 1960s.

Lamé: fabric that is interwoven with metallic threads.

Leggings: footless leg covering created from elastic material in the 1980s

Liberty: British fashion and textile firm famous for its cotton floral prints

Louvre pleats: pleats running horizontally.

Mandarin (or Chinese, or Nehru) collar: stand-up collar that is open at the front.

Maxi skirt: ankle- or floor-length skirt popular around 1970.

Midiskirt: calf-length skirt; although this term is no longer in use, the length itself has been dominant since 1973.

Military style: often in khaki, this look is inspired by military uniforms.

Miniskirt: a very short skirt, with the minimum distance between hem and knee being 10 cm (4 in).

Moiré: generally used for formal eveningwear, this is a watered effect or fabric; formerly silk and also acetate.

Nautical style: leisure- and sportswear style, usually in navy blue and white, and modelled on naval uniforms.

New Look (Corolle line): world-famous silhouette created in 1947 by Christian Dior. Very feminine with narrow, rounded shoulders, narrow waist, emphasized bust and wide, calf-length skirt.

Nylon: patented in the USA in 1937 and initially used in the manufacture of hosiery and underwear.

Op Art: art style typified by abstract, geometric patterns and bold colours, especially black and white; a major influence in 1960s fashion.

Organdy: lightweight, fine, sheer and stiffened cotton (now synthetic), usually in pastel shades.

Organza: similar to organdy, this fabric was originally made of silk.

Oversize look: garments that appear several sizes too large; fashionable in the 1980s.

Pagoda shoulder: launched in 1933 by Elsa Schiaparelli, this emphasized shoulder was inspired by Asian pagodas.

Paletot: single- or double-breasted coat with patch pockets and lapels.

Panniers: structured undergarment or hoops that extended the width of the dress to both sides while leaving the front and back flat. Popular in the eighteenth century, modified versions have appeared since then.

Parallelo: very fashionable in the 1950s, this is a horizontally knitted sweater or jacket.

Passementerie: generic term used to describe all kinds of garment trimmings, essential requirements for Coco Chanel's suits.

Passe-partout jacket: similar to a bolero.

Pencil line: figure-hugging style created by Christian Dior in 1948, whereby the skirt is cut from the hips in one straight line.

Pennant collar: triangular shaped collar.

Pepita: small, checked and woven pattern with diagonal connecting lines, usually in navy and white, or black and white.

Peplum jacket: short tailored jacket with flared flaps or flounces sewn into the waist.

Peter Pan collar: rounded, small flat collar.

Piqué: cotton fabric with a relief pattern; usually waffled or honeycombed.

Pinafore dress: collarless, sleeveless dress based on a chasuble.

Plissé: term used to describe pleats that are pressed into fabric.

Princess line: coat or dress without a waist seam; tailoring is achieved by working in the vertical seam. Launched in 1863 by Charles Frederick Worth, popular again 1900, in the 1930s and then again between 1955 and 1965.

Puff sleeves: gathered above the elbow, this is a balloon-like short sleeve.

Puffball or pouf skirt: created by Christian Lacroix in the 1980s, the skirt is doubled over at the hem to create a puffed appearance.

Pullover: woollen, long-sleeved top inspired by the knitted garments worn by seamen. Popular in 1920s Europe, when Coco Chanel included it in several of her haute couture collections.

Raglan sleeve: a sleeve extending from the neckline to the wrist.

Rayon: a name for viscose used between the early 1950s and the 1970s.

Redingote: tailored long jacket or coat, usually flared toward the hem and often with a shawl collar. It can be worn with or without a belt.

Revers: lapels; sometimes refers to the turned-over edge of sleeves or skirts.

Romantic look: 1960s and 1970s style of dress, incorporating folk elements and featuring loose cotton dresses, frills and corset tops.

Sabrina neckline: inspired by Audrey Hepburn's clothes in the movie of the same name, this is a square, décolleté collar.

Safari jacket: jacket in a strong, lightweight fabric that is modelled on tropical garments. It is characterized by the colours brown, beige and khaki, and by patch pockets and shoulder flaps. Usually fitted with a belt.

Sailor collar: neckline and collar inspired by naval uniforms.

Sailor neck: zip-fastened turtleneck.

Shantung: irregular, less shiny silk; hand-woven.

Sheath dress: usually knee-length classic dress, collarless and close-fitting, straight and cut from a single fabric piece, with a round or oval neckline; also an evening dress with shoulder straps and décolleté; popular in the 1920s, in the 1960s it became known as the 'Jackie O dress' (after Jacqueline Kennedy Onassis).

Shelf bra: a bra that is built into the garment.

Shift dress: loosely falling, unstructured classic style of dress especially fashionable during the 1920s and mid-1960s.

Shirtwaister: the upper part of this loose dress is modelled on a man's shirt, with a collar, cuffs and buttons to the waist. Popularized by Coco Chanel.

Slinky look: originally fashionable in the 1930s and later revived in the early 1970s; a phrase used to describe sinuous clothes of fluid fabrics.

Slit look: a miniskirt or hot pants worn beneath a midi- or maxiskirt left open at the front; fashionable in the early 1970s.

Smock: narrow, straight dress with front, back and sleeves secured to a yoke collar.

Smocking: fabric tightly gathered with decorative stitching (often created with elastic thread) to form geometric patterns; frequently featured in peasant-style garments.

Spencer: waist-length, short jacket.

Sportswear: generic term to describe comfortable leisurewear.

Swing coat: style of A-line coat, with narrow sleeves and shoulders; shorter than knee-length.

Taffeta: stiffened fine fabric of synthetic fibres or silk often made of changeant (an iridescent material).

Tea gown: loose gown designed in 1864 by Charles Frederick Worth with an intricately decorated front and long sleeves.

Topper: straight, short jacket with sloping shoulders, the front edge forms a right angle with the hem.

Torso dress: simple dress that is gathered or pleated below the hipline with a figure-hugging bodice.

Trapeze line: silhouette of coat or dress with narrow shoulders and a high waist (or no waist at all) flaring out towards the hem. Yves Saint Laurent presented his trapeze line in 1958 and it remained popular through the 1960s.

Tube: garment with a straight, elongated outline that is cut in a casual and comfortable way.

Tulle: lace-like or netting fabric.

Tunic: simple pinafore or dress in a loose, often sleeveless style; the armholes usually form part of the side seams.

Tweed: rough-textured, woollen fabric in a variety of coloured patterns; used especially for suits and coats.

Twist line: narrow-hipped outline with a slightly flared pleated skirt that flares as the wearer moves about.

Umbrella skirt: like an umbrella, this skirt consists of 12 or more sections.

U-neckline: neckline in a U-shape with wide shoulder straps.

V-neck: neckline with an open yoke coming to a V shape midway down the bodice.

Velvet: soft-textured, short-piled fabric; usually cotton.

Vichy check: checked pattern that is like gingham but with larger checks.

Viennese seam: a seam running from one armhole angled across the bust to either the hem or the waist seam, obviating the need for darts.

Viscose: synthetic fibre made of cellulose.

Voile: lightweight, sheer fabric.

Westover: worn with suits in the 1920s and more recently over skirts and blouses, this is a sleeveless, knitted waistcoat.

Wing collar: collar with upper corners covering shoulder seams.

Y-line: garment line designed in 1955–56 by Christian Dior featuring narrow dresses or skirts, wide lapels or other V-shaped necklines to form the letter 'Y'.

Further Reading

Aloha Attire: Hawaiian Dress in the 20th Century, Linda B Arthur Atglen, Schiffer, 2000.

The Art of Zandra Rhodes, Zandra Rhodes/Anne Knight, Jonathan Cape, 1984.

California Casual, Maureen Reilly, PA Schiffer Ltd, 2001.

The Conscription of Fashion: Utility Cloth, Clothing and Footwear, 1941–1952, Christopher Sladen, Scolar Press, 1995.

The Couture Accessory, Caroline Rennolds Milbank, HN Abrams, 2002.

Everyday Fashions of the Thirties As Pictured in Sears Catalogs, Sears Roebuck & Company, Courier Dover Publications, 1986.

The Fashion Year, edited by Brenda Polan, Zomba Books, 1983.

The Fashion Year Volume II, edited by Emily White, Zomba Books, 1984.

Fashions of a Decade: 1940s, Patricia Baker, Batsford, 1992.

A History of Fashion, Elizabeth Ewing, Batsford, 2005.

Hollywood Costume: Glamour, Glitter & Romance, Dale McConathy with Diana Vreeland, HN Abrams, 1976.

Hollywood Knits, Bill Gibb, Pavilion Books, 1987.

In Biba, Delisia Howard, Chris Price and Barbara Hulanicki, Hazard Books, 2004.

In Fashion, Prudence Glynn/Madeline Ginsburg, George Allen & Unwin Ltd, 1978.

In Vogue: Sixty Years of Celebrities and Fashion from British Vogue, Georgina Howell, Penguin Books, 1978.

New York Fashion, Caroline Rennolds Milbank, Abrams, 1989.

The 1940s, John Peacock, Thames & Hudson, 1998.

NOVA 1965–1975, compiled by David Hillman and Harriet Peccinotti, edited by David Gibbs, Pavilion Books, 1993.

The Ossie Clark Diaries, Lady Henrietta Rous, Bloomsbury, 1998.

Ossie Clark 1965–74, Judith Watt, V&A Publications, 2003.

Print in Fashion, Marnie Fogg, Batsford Books, 2006.

Schiaparelli Fashion Review, Tom Tierney, Dover Publications Inc, 1988.

Screen Style: Fashion and Femininity in 1930s Hollywood, Sarah Berry, University of Minnesota Press, 2002.

Twentieth-Century Fashion, Linda Watson, Carlton Books, 1999.

Vanitas: Designs By Gianni Versace, Hamish Bowles, Abbeville Press, 1994

Picture Credits

The publishers would like to thank the following sources for their kind permission to reproduce the photographs in this book.
Key: t=Top, b=Bottom, c=Centre, l=Left and r=Right

The Advertising Archive Ltd: 37, 41c

Camera Press: /David Steen: 32

Corbis: /Bettmann: 8tl, 8cr, 22cl, 22tr, 28tr, 34cl, 35tr, 35bl, 40cr/© Condé Nast Archive: 6, 13, 14, 16cl, 19, 20, 22bl, 22cr, 23tr, 24, 25, 26, 30, 41cl; /Julio Donoso/Corbis Sygma: 46; /Lynn Goldsmith: 48r; / Historical Picture Archive: 28; /Hulton-Deutsch Collection: 9tr, 17cl, 17bl, 29tr, 66; /David Lees: 28l;/ Genevieve Naylor: 23bl

Getty Images: /H.Armstrong Roberts/Retrofile: 41bl; /Hulton Archive: 49tr;/Sasha: 16tr; /Topical Press Agency: 9c; /United Artists: 40bl; /William Vanderson/Fox Photos: 16cr

© **Norman Parkinson Archive:** 38

Rex Features: /Europa Press: 84cr; /Everett Collection: 29bl, 34bl

TopFoto.co.uk: 9cl, 28cr, 35tl, 41cr, 48l, 49bl; /AP: 29tl

Victoria & Albert Museum: 45

Every effort has been made to acknowledge correctly and contact the source and/or copyright holder of each picture and Carlton Books Limited apologizes for any unintentional errors or omissions which will be corrected in future editions of this book.

Acknowledgements

Emma Baxter-Wright: Special thanks to Lisa Dyer for commissioning me. Dedicated to Dex, O and Dusty Rose. **Karen Clarkson:** Dedicated to Nisse Sauerland, Simon Swift and Hector, with love. **Sarah Kennedy:** Thanks to Lisa Helmanis, Emma Hodges, Carol McKeown and Jane W. Kellock for fashion memories and positive inspiration. Dedicated to Duncan, Freddie and Findlay, with love. **Kate Mulvey:** Dedicated to Georgia, Myles, George and Oscar, with love.

The publishers would especially like to thank Cleo and Mark Butterfield for their hospitality, warmth and enthusiasm during the photography process, and particularly for their vast knowledge and expertise in helping to select from their amazing fashion archives. Thanks also go to Zandra Rhodes, fo her rare artistry and fervent dedication to fashion heritage. Thanks to Bang Bang Clothing Exchange, 21 Goodge Street, London W1T 2PJ and Rellik, 3 Goldbourne Road, Notting Hill, London W10 5NW.